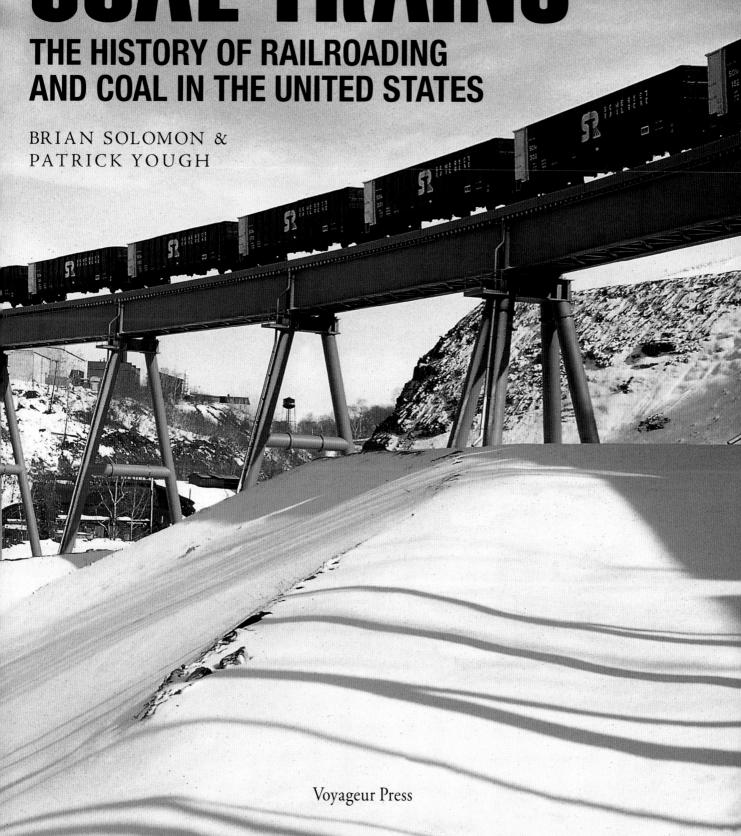

COAL TRAINS

THE HISTORY OF RAILROADING AND COAL IN THE UNITED STATES

BRIAN SOLOMON &
PATRICK YOUGH

Voyageur Press

Dedication

To James & Betty Yough

First published in 2009 by Voyageur Press, an imprint of MBI Publishing Company, 400 First Avenue North, Suite 300, Minneapolis, MN 55401 USA

Voyageur Press titles are also available at discounts in bulk quantity for industrial or sales-promotional use. For details write to Special Sales Manager at MBI Publishing Company, 400 First Avenue North, Suite 300, Minneapolis, MN 55401 USA.

To find out more about our books, visit us online at www.voyageurpress.com.

Library of Congress Cataloging-in-Publication Data

Solomon, Brian, 1966–
    Coal trains : the history of railroading and coal in the United States / Brian Solomon & Patrick Yough.
        p. cm.
    Includes bibliographical references and index.
    ISBN 978-0-7603-3359-4 (hb w/ jkt)
    1. Mine railroad trains—United States—History. 2. Mine railroads—United States—History. 3. Coal mines and mining—United States—History. I. Yough, Patrick. II. Title.
    TN336.S64 2009
    385.5'40973—dc22
                                                    2009001324

On the front cover: Today, American railroads move coal in long unit trains operating with dedicated sets of equipment directly from mines to power plants. In October 2005, a pair of CSX SD70MACs leads a unit train leaving Acca Yard in Richmond, Virginia. *Brian Solomon*

On the frontis: The Reading Company proclaimed itself America's largest anthracite carrier. As the volume of anthracite declined, Reading retained a greater portion of this traditional traffic than did other anthracite railroads. *Reading Company, Railroad Museum of Pennsylvania PHMC*

On the title page: In 1983, New York State Electric & Gas opened the 15-mile Somerset Railroad to serve the new 684-megawatt Somerset generating station on the shore of Lake Ontario northeast of Lockport. The most impressive infrastructure on the new line is this modern trestle constructed on a 19.5-degree banked curve. In 1999, both the generating station and the railroad were sold to the AES Corporation. *Don Rohauer*

On the table of contents: Loaded unit train symbol 04TT224 from Powder River Basin's Black Thunder Mine is destined for Wisconsin Public Service at Weston, Wisconsin, south of Wausau. On January 28, 1989, it works past Toluca between Gillette, Wyoming, and Billings, Montana, on Burlington Northern's Big Horn Subdivision. BN assigned homebuilt fuel tenders to reduce the need for fueling coal trains in remote areas. *John Leopard*

On the back cover: Union Pacific train CJOBT9-29 starts into the loading loop at the Black Thunder Mine. The train took slightly over an hour to load and departed symbol CBTJO9-03, destined for the Electric Energy plant in Joppa, Illinois. The cars are lettered for Ameren Energy subsidiary Joppa & Eastern Railroad. Ameren is the majority owner in Electric Energy and in 2006 was the largest buyer of Powder River coal. *Patrick Yough*

Editor: Dennis Pernu
Designer: Wendy R. Lutge
Jacket Designer: idesign, inc., Chicago, IL

Printed in China

TABLE OF CONTENTS

INTRODUCTION

Glinting aluminum empties passing below the hulk of the old locomotive coaling tower at DeKalb, Illinois, present a symbolic image of the long ties between coal and railroading and how the relationship has evolved. At one time, coal was the primary fuel for locomotives, industry, and home heating. Today, most coal is mined for consumption by electric utilities. When Chicago & North Western built this gigantic coaling tower to fuel locomotives on its east-west main line, the movement of Powder River unit trains was still decades in the future. *Brian Solomon*

Coal and railways have a long, intertwined relationship. Coal made the railways, and the railways made coal.

The rise of coal as a heating fuel in seventeenth- and eighteenth-century Britain resulted in more efficient methods of mining and transporting it. Short colliery tram lines using wooden rails and wagons hauled by pack animals were an antecedent to railway lines. As mines reached deeper, they filled with water, necessitating the development of more effective pumps. Key to the invention of the steam engine was the evolutionary jump from a simple vacuum pump to a steam pump. Thomas Newcomen, a Cornish blacksmith born in 1663, perfected Thomas Savery's suction engine and successfully built a steam-actuated pump applying low-pressure steam to a piston in a sealed cylinder. The engine was enormous and ponderously slow—it worked at only four or five strokes per minute. As Newcomen and others perfected and refined the stationary steam engine, dozens were built at locations across the coal-mining regions of Britain. In time, more uses for the steam engine were devised, and it became a key instrument in powering Britain's Industrial Revolution. Yet it took nearly another century for the stationary engine to evolve into a self-propelled steam locomotive.

In 1803, engine designer Richard Trevithick constructed the first full-sized locomotive designed to run on rails. This was demonstrated at the Pen-y-Darran Iron Works in Wales on February 13, 1804. Over the next two decades, the steam-powered railway emerged in Britain as a new form of transport. Initially, steam railways were an outgrowth of the early tram lines and were closely linked to collieries and other industrial complexes. The first common carrier (or public) railway—as opposed to a single-purpose industrial tram—was the 12-mile Stockton & Darlington. Authorized by an act of parliament in 1821, it was also the first such railway to use steam locomotives, thanks to its engineer, George Stephenson. This line, and Stephenson's more ambitious Liverpool & Manchester of 1829, established the pattern for railway building across Britain and ultimately around the world.

The DL&W four-wheel car pictured here was typical of Pennsylvania anthracite lines in the first decades of coal haulage. Author Thomas Taber notes that when the railroad began moving anthracite in the 1850s, it was a primitive line, and coal was moved in wood-sided four-wheel cars called coal jimmies, with a capacity of just 6 to 8 tons each. By the 1880s, the railroad had adopted more robust eight-wheel wood-sided hoppers, each carrying 20 tons. *T. T. Taber collection, Railroad Museum of Pennsylvania PHMC*

A rare view from the mid-nineteenth century depicts a Philadelphia & Reading 0-6-0 locomotive at the Frackville, Pennsylvania, scale office. The locomotive was identified by noted author John H. White (in a letter to former Railroad Museum of Pennsylvania director George Hart) as resembling one of Baldwin's unusual flexible-beam engines built in the 1850s. In the years prior to the American Civil War, P&R was the largest freight hauler in the United States, and the bulk of its business was anthracite. *Railroad Museum of Pennsylvania PHMC*

The United States was quick to follow Britain's lead, and in the 1820s, U.S. engineers traveled to Britain to study and import the technology necessary to build and operate steam railways in the United States. As in Britain, many of the earliest U.S. railways were built specifically for the transport of coal. In the 1830s, railway-building accelerated and was a key to sparking America's first Industrial Revolution, which mimicked its British counterpart and resulted in the development of intensive coal-mining and iron industries in eastern Pennsylvania. Perfection of the railroad fueled the rapid spread of these industries; not only did railroads facilitate the movement of coal and iron ores, they were also the largest consumers of both coal and iron. By the late nineteenth century the coal-fired locomotive was the symbol of progress and commonplace across North America. Iron industries in eastern Pennsylvania gradually gave birth to a full-blown industrial economy, and an intensive steel industry emerged in western Pennsylvania, eastern Ohio, and elsewhere.

Coal was burned for industrial purposes and was integral in the manufacturing of steel. It was also a preferred home-heating fuel and was moved in large volumes to growing urban areas, especially in the Northeast. As a nonperishable, heavy-mineral bulk commodity, coal typically followed the most efficient and least costly means of transport. From the earliest days this usually resulted in a mix of water and railway transport.

Early coal railways initially fed inland waterways and canal heads. Later lines delivered coal to Great Lakes and Atlantic seaports. Coal traffic moving in large volumes over well-established routes became the cash cow for many railways, and since the earliest days of U.S. railroading it consistently has been a primary source of railway revenue. Routes serving coal-producing areas have been some of heaviest built and busiest lines in the country.

During the twentieth century, coal usage underwent dramatic changes. As the internal combustion engine was refined and an oil-based economy devel-

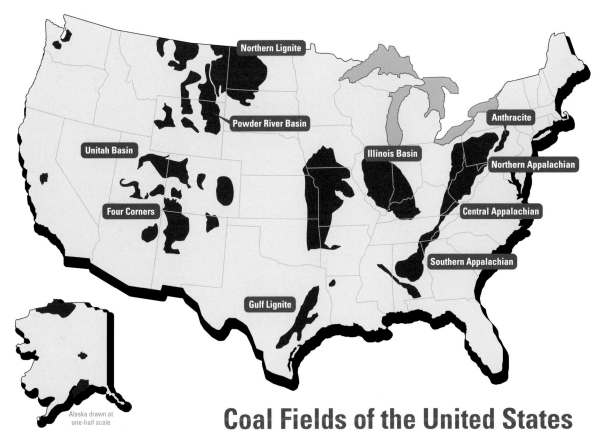

Coal Fields of the United States

oped, petroleum products began to replace coal as a primary fuel for both transport and home heating. First to suffer were the anthracite lines of eastern Pennsylvania, where from the late 1920s onward the high cost of mining, supply disruptions resulting from inequitable labor policies, and other problems resulted in the loss of traffic. Although bituminous coal didn't suffer the same level of market devastation, it was also largely abandoned as a home-heating fuel during the middle decades of the twentieth century and lost traffic as a result of declines in American heavy industry. However, important new markets for bituminous coal emerged as the old ones faded.

The electrification of North America in the first decades of the twentieth century produced a voracious demand for coal never imagined by visionaries of the early Industrial Revolution.

Coal-fired electric-generating stations—power plants emerged as the largest consumers of bituminous coal. As electrical consumption increased, it drove an ever greater need for coal, much of it delivered from mine to plant by railways. The export market, of little importance before World War I, grew rapidly after the war, then soared after World War II. Coal from Appalachian mines flowed in torrents to Atlantic ports, both for foreign export and for movement to domestic coastal power plants.

In recent decades, the mining, movement, and consumption of coal have been affected by fluctuations (and disruptions) in the global energy market and measures imposed by air-quality legislation. Concerns about air pollution resulted in legislation that produced important changes on the types of coal consumed, and thus where coal is mined.

COAL MOVING OUT OF WYOMING FILLS AS MANY AS 76 TRAINS PER DAY, SOME WEIGHING MORE THAN 18,000 TONS.

Today the largest sources of North American coal are Wyoming mines where low-sulfur coal (compliant with strict modern air-quality regulations) is easily mined for shipment to power plants across the country. In 2007, Wyoming accounted for the 10 largest mines in the United States, which produced more than 413 million tons of the 1.1 billion tons mined in the United States that year. The coal moving out of Wyoming fills as many as 76 trains per day, some weighing more than 18,000 tons.

In the early days of coal railroading, the commodity was moved in small four-wheel cars called jimmies, each carrying roughly 8 tons of coal, with whole trainloads weighing just 150 tons. The gradual improvement of railway lines, bridges, motive power, and braking and signaling systems has allowed ever-greater efficiency through ever-larger cars and longer and much heavier trains. Today, aluminum cars can carry up to 125 tons of coal each, and most trains range between 105 to 135 cars. On some lines coal trains weigh in excess of 21,000 tons.

A crucial innovation in modern coal transport was the development of the unit train. Traditionally,

B&O's EM-1s weighed just 628,700 pounds, yet they were the largest locomotives ever to operate on the Baltimore & Ohio, featuring 118-sqare-foot firebox grates and providing 115,000 pounds of tractive effort. Baldwin built 30 of these simple articulated locomotives during World War II, and they tended to work the heavily graded lines west of Cumberland, Maryland. It was overcast on October 19, 1947, when EM-1 No. 7613 led 80 coal cars through Terra Alta, West Virginia. *Bruce Fales, Jay Williams collection*

TODAY, ALUMINUM CARS CAN CARRY UP TO 125 TONS OF COAL EACH, AND MOST TRAINS RANGE BETWEEN 105 TO 135 CARS.

Opposite: On May 5, 1957, PRR Class I1s No. 4414 leads a loaded coal train on the Elmira Branch at Roaring Branch, Pennsylvania. The coal is destined for the Lake Ontario pier at Sodus Point, New York. *Jim Shaughnessy*

small mines loaded individual cars. As late as 1958, all railroad-hauled coal was billed by the carload. These carloads were collected by mine runs, then sorted and assembled into larger trains for shipment over long distances. Often, cars were classified several times at large yards before reaching their destination. This had evolved from the days when many coal customers used a carload of coal or less. Even where large volumes of coal were loaded into ships, the cars of a single train may have been loaded by a dozen mines. The unit train speeded

IN 2007, WYOMING'S NORTH ANTELOPE ROCHELLE MINE PRODUCED 91.5 MILLION TONS—MORE COAL THAN THE COMBINED PRODUCTION OF THE TOP 50 MINES IN 1958.

delivery and lowered transportation costs through economies of scale. Whole trains now moved directly from mine to customer and eliminated the need to switch and classify cars at intermediate yards. In 1964, New York Central advertised that its unit trains cut costs by 30 percent.

The unit train was made possible by several changes to mining, consumption, and railroad transport specifically, the advent of very large shippers and large customers combined with ability to load and unload cars quickly. Keys were new enormous

Above: Steel Conrail coal hoppers glide under a signal bridge on the former Pennsylvania Railroad main line. In its day, PRR was among the leading carriers of bituminous coal. *Scott R. Snell*

Opposite: An eastbound Southern Railway unit coal train rolls through Oreton, Virginia, en route to a coal-fired generating station in either North or South Carolina. The Southern is generally credited with inventing the unit train in order to overcome competition from government-subsidized barge transport. *Ron Flanary*

modern mines with bulk-loading facilities capable of loading a whole train in a relatively short span of time, as well as the construction of massive generating stations and modern transshipping facilities. The dramatic increase of mine output helps put the role of the unit train in perspective. In 1958, on the eve of the unit train, the largest coal mine in the country was U.S. Steel's Robena C facility in Pennsylvania, built in 1946, that produced 3.5 million tons a year. (At that time, most of the top 50 mines in the nation produced between 1 and 2 million tons annually.) In 2007, America's most productive mine, Wyoming's North Antelope Rochelle Mine, produced 91.5 million tons, more coal than the combined production of the top 50 mines in 1958. Each of the top 50 mines in 2007 produced more than 4 million tons. In 1958 the top 50 mines produced slightly more than 20 percent of the total volume of coal mined; in 2007, the top 50 mines produced 64 percent of the coal. The trend has been toward much larger mines that produce a much greater volume of coal and a larger percentage of the total coal mined.

An eastbound loaded Burlington Northern Santa Fe coal train ascends Crawford Hill at Breezy Point, Nebraska, on October 5, 2003. *Howard Ande*

Southern Railway pioneered the unit coal train concept. Burke Davis, author of *The Southern Railway: Road of the Innovators*, explained the railroad's innovation. In the late 1950s, the Southern, like many American railroads, was suffering from declining traffic and a loss of market share, so it sought means to lower its costs in order to deliver coal at lower rates and thus better compete with other modes. Specifically, Southern looked to move coal from southern Alabama mines near Jasper to a large new generating station being built at Wilsonville, Alabama, that would require an estimated 10,000 tons of coal daily. Under the supervision of Southern's visionary vice president of operations, D. W. Brosnan (later president), the solution was worked out by principal innovators L. Stanley Crane and Bob Hamilton, who devised an arrangement to use a fleet of new large-capacity aluminum hoppers designed for rapid loading and rapid discharge. These were operated in solid dedicated trains that ran directly from the mines to the new power plant. Burke notes that by keeping the cars together, equipment utilization was improved "six or seven times the normal rate."

Rio Grande No. 5372 leads coal loads at the Tri-States generating station at Craig, Colorado, on June 19, 1992. *John Leopard*

Today most coal is moved by dedicated unit trains of 105 cars or more. Modern unit trains of nearly identical aluminum cars snaking though the landscape behind state-of-the-art, high-horsepower, low-emissions, diesel-electric locomotives have become a symbol of modern railroading.

This book covers many elements of coal train operation over the years, from the formative anthracite haulers in Pennsylvania to the latest developments in Appalachian coal country and Wyoming's Powder River Basin. Yet, the long history and great complexity of coal operations means a book of this nominal size can be no more than a cursory overview of operations. Even if this book covered 8 or 10 volumes it could only scratch the surface of American coal railroading. Many different railroads are discussed, and many of the largest and best-known coal lines are profiled, but it has not been our intention to detail every coal-hauling line. Still, we hope to have captured the flavor, spirit, and history of coal train operation in the United States.

398-A

SLOAN BREAKER
D. L. & W.

Chapter 1
THE ANTHRACITE HAULERS

Anthracite coal breakers once dotted the northeastern Pennsylvania landscape. These facilities crushed coal into usable pieces, separated burnable coal from other minerals, then loaded them into coal cars for transport. This view of Delaware, Lackawanna & Western's Sloan Breaker dates from the early twentieth century. Sloan processed coal from the Clark vein. In later years it was known as the Moffatt Breaker, operated by the Moffatt Coal Company. *T. T. Taber collection, Railroad Museum of Pennsylvania PHMC*

The rolling mountains of eastern Pennsylvania encompass one of the world's foremost deposits of anthracite, commonly known as "hard coal." The four principal anthracite fields are located in northeastern Pennsylvania between the Susquehanna and Delaware rivers. Although anthracite was known in the eighteenth century and burned in small quantities in eastern cities, it wasn't until the early nineteenth century that anthracite was valued commercially as fuel. Once ignited, anthracite burns hot and clean, making it desirable for both industrial applications and home heating. In their book *Kingdom of Coal*, authors Donald L. Miller and Richard E. Sharpless point out that as early as 1812–1813 Baltimore was consuming 7,000 to 10,000 tons of coal annually.

America's first coal boom was set into motion by Josiah White and Erskine Hazard, Pennsylvania industrialists credited with developing an effective method for burning anthracite and for early commercial development of anthracite mines.

Anthracite tends to form at extreme angles to the surface and is typically wedged between thick layers of sedimentary rock, making it difficult to mine. To extract it from the ground required deep shafts and substantial tunnel networks that were worked by armies of miners. Above ground, extensive breakers were necessary to crush the coal—or "black diamonds"—into usable-sized pieces and remove mineral waste.

White and Hazard formed the Lehigh Coal and Lehigh Navigation Companies (later consolidated as the Lehigh Coal and Navigation Company) to mine and distribute anthracite. Initially they harnessed natural waterways, and later man-made canals, shipping anthracite in simple boats to urban markets. In 1820, the populations of American cities were tiny by today's measure: New York had just 150,000 residents, Philadelphia less than 64,000. As cities grew, so did the demand for coal. To deliver more coal, better transportation was needed, and Hazard was among the Americans who traveled to Britain in the mid-1820s to learn about improved transport, including steam railways.

In its day, the Delaware & Hudson Gravity Railroad was an intensive industrial complex devised to move anthracite to the canal head at Honesdale, Pennsylvania. This period view of the Racket Brook Breaker, located at the gravity line's Plane No. 4, depicts a host of eight-wheel wooden coal cars. Cables moved by stationary engines hauled cars upgrade. *W. A. Lucas collection, Railroad Museum of Pennsylvania PHMC*

Canals and Gravity Railways

The gravity railway built at Mauch Chunk (a town on the Lehigh River known today as Jim Thorpe) is often credited as the first coal railway in the United States. It was created to fulfill White and Hazard's need to connect their mines at Summit Hill with a growing transport hub at Mauch Chunk. Based in part on British prototypes, they built a nameless gravity railroad during 1827 using wooden strap-iron rails. It was just 9 miles long. Loaded mine cars, each carrying approximately 1.5 tons of coal, were hauled to the top of a grade by pack animals, and from there they rolled—by gravity—the remaining distance to the Mauch Chunk canal terminal. On the downgrade, speed was regulated by a brakeman using a primitive handbrake. At the terminal the cars dumped coal into boats for shipment downriver. Originally the empty coal cars were hauled by animals back upgrade to the mines, but in the mid-1840s the railway was substantially modified with the installation of an ingenious back-track system of switchbacks and inclined planes. Stationary engines and ropes were employed to hoist cars up exceptionally steep grades, speeding the return of empties and eliminating the need for animal power. Known in later years as the Switchback, this formative railway hauled coal for more than two generations and inspired similar enterprises elsewhere in Pennsylvania. Although the Switchback lost its usefulness as a coal conveyor after 1872, it continued to operate as a tourist attraction until the early 1930s.

In the days of fountain pens, coal dealers often gave out
blotters that advertised the type of coal they sold.
Patrick Yough collection

In 1823 the Delaware & Hudson Canal
Company was chartered to move anthracite from
underground mines at Carbondale, Pennsylvania, to
the New York market. Like the Mauch Chunk line,
D&H sent an engineer to Britain to study railways
and imported technology back to the United States.
In conjunction with its 108-mile-long canal, D&H
constructed a 17-mile-long gravity railway with
strap-iron rails during 1828–1829. The railway was
designed to move coal from mines near Carbondale
over the mountains to a canal head at Honesdale,
Pennsylvania. Anticipating locomotive haulage
on level sections, D&H imported British-made
locomotives—widely known as the first full-size
commercial steam locomotives in the United
States—but the weight of the engines made regular
operation impractical, and D&H instead relied
on animal power, inclined planes with stationary
engines, and gravity power.

D&H profited greatly from the growing
demand for anthracite, and its operations were a key
to the development of the home-heating market.
The company continued to expand its operations,
eventually evolving into a conventional railroad
using steam locomotive haulage. D&H's railroad
lines reached south to Scranton and Wilkes-Barre,
where it tapped mines and interchanged with other
lines, and northward to markets in New York state,

New England, and Canada. The original D&H
canal and gravity railroad survived for 70 years,
with the last coal boat navigating the canal on
November 5, 1898, and the gravity railroad shutting
down shortly thereafter.

Coal, Railroads, and Industrial Revolution

Increased demand for coal led to the success of
canals and early gravity railroads while spurring
America's first Industrial Revolution. This in turn
inspired America's first railroad-building frenzy.
In the years prior to the American Civil War, the
anthracite boom fueled an intensive iron-making
industry in eastern Pennsylvania. Boomtowns like
Scranton, Reading, Bethlehem, and Allentown grew
around iron mines, furnaces, and foundries.

Crucial to rapid railroad expansion was the
perfection of the steam locomotive. The locomotive
fueled its fire with a forced draft from exhausting
cylinders that caused the fire to burn hotter and the
boiler to generate greater amounts of steam as the
locomotive gained speed. As the primary movers
of iron and coal, the steam railroads' success made
production and delivery of commercial iron cheaper
than ever before. Yet, railroads were also the primary
consumers of both coal and iron, so as they expanded,

Animal-hauled tram railways were among the precursors
to the development of full-service steam railways. This
nineteenth-century mule-drawn tram line in a Pennsylvania
anthracite mine mimics the practices adopted in Britain
centuries earlier. *Railroad Museum of Pennsylvania PHMC*

Electrification of anthracite tram railways improved the efficiency with which coal was extracted from the ground and eliminated the need for horses. This view of a Pennsylvania anthracite mine dates from about 1910. *Railroad Museum of Pennsylvania PHMC*

they fueled demand for both commodities. After the Civil War, the iron industry was gradually supplanted by the steel industry, but railroads remained integral to coal mining and steel production.

Although first built to serve canal heads, anthracite railways ultimately superseded canals. The growing voracious demand for coal encouraged competing commercial interests to build myriad and often duplicative railway systems to tap mines and serve industrial and domestic markets. Railroad interests vied with one another for territory and traffic in the anthracite region, building overlapping routes in what emerged as one of the most intensely developed rail networks in the United States.

Philadelphia & Reading

Incorporated to connect its namesake cities on April 4, 1833, Philadelphia & Reading was engineered by early master of railroad building Moncure Robinson. Envisioned as an anthracite hauler, the line opened to Philadelphia in December 1839. In his comprehensive book, *American Railroad Freight Car*, John H. White Jr. writes that P&R's first year of full-scale freight operations was in 1842 and that at that time it moved 6,000 tons weekly over its 90-mile line between the Pottsville mining hub and Philadelphia. Jay V. Hare, in his *History of the Reading*, writes that P&R's line to Philadelphia's Port Richmond docks opened on May 17, 1842. He details an early move, saying, "On May 21 a train of 50 cars containing 150 tons of coal from the mines of Gideon Bast were forwarded to Port Richmond."

P&R's business grew rapidly, and by 1855 it was moving 2 million tons of anthracite annually. The

Reading Company's Port Richmond car dumper in Philadelphia, Pennsylvania. Note the rider at the back of the hopper: as the car rolls into position by gravity, he will control the speed by setting the handbrake. In 1960, Reading set a record at Port Richmond by dumping 495 anthracite hoppers carrying 29,100 tons of coal in a single day. *Reading Company, Railroad Museum of Pennsylvania PHMC*

Reading Company 61171 was an eight-wheel wood-sided coal hopper, part of an order for 1,000 cars (Nos. 60000–60999) constructed in 1902 and rebuilt in 1921. In the form shown here, each was rated to carry up to 40 tons of coal. By comparison, Reading's older eight-wheel cars had evolved from 10-ton capacity in the 1880s to 30-ton capacity by the early twentieth century. Car 61171 is pictured after being brought into compliance with the U.S. Safety Appliance Standards. *Reading Company, Railroad Museum of Pennsylvania PHMC*

importance of coal was paramount to the railway, at the time one of the most successful in the world. White notes that in 1859 P&R was the largest freight hauler (of any mode) in the United States. In the nineteenth century, P&R came to dominate transportation in southern anthracite fields as it built, bought, leased, and controlled lines. Its routes covered the anthracite region from the lower Delaware to Susquehanna rivers. It reached north from Philadelphia to Allentown and Bethlehem, and northwest of Reading, Pennsylvania, to serve dozens of coal-producing towns, including

In the nineteenth century, an intensive industry developed around the mining of anthracite coal in eastern Pennsylvania. This glass-plate view shows the top of an inclined plane on the Philadelphia & Reading where stationary engines were used to haul freight cars up exceptionally steep gradients with metal cables. P&R operated several inclines, including the Gordon and Mahanoy planes. Virtually none of this type of infrastructure has survived into modern times. *Railroad Museum of Pennsylvania PHMC*

Pottsville, Mahanoy City, Tamaqua, and Shamokin. Furthermore, P&R reached beyond the anthracite fields to secure both all-rail connections and new markets for its coal. Lines ran southwest via Harrisburg to Lurgan and Gettysburg to interchange with the Western Maryland; west and northwest to Newberry Junction near Williamsport to interchange with the Fallbrook Route (later New York Central); and northeast across New Jersey to its Atlantic port at

Port Reading (on the Arthur Kill opposite Staten Island) to reach the New York market. In the late nineteenth century, P&R's officers had dreams of a virtual anthracite monopoly. By that time its lines blanketed some 75 percent of the mining region, and it was by far the largest mover of anthracite coal.

In 1883, P&R took control of Central Railroad of New Jersey. It temporarily lost that control as a result of financial distress, but the two lines would remain closely related. P&R was reorganized as the Reading Company in 1893, and by 1901, Reading was again in control of CNJ. Their systems complemented each other well: CNJ tapped northern anthracite fields and routed traffic east to New York and New England, while Reading served the southern and central fields, directing coal to Philadelphia and west via New York Central, the Pennsylvania Railroad, and the Western Maryland. Together,

Conrail-era spinoff Reading, Blue Mountain & Northern, known today as Reading & Northern, has continued to serve the anthracite industry in the spirit of the great nineteenth-century Pennsylvania coal haulers. On April 23, 1991, U33B No. 3301 rests with hoppers at the Kocher Ramp in Goodspring, Pennsylvania, at the end of the former Reading Company Goodspring Branch accessed via Port Clinton. During the 1990s, RBM&N/R&N expanded services in eastern Pennsylvania on lines shed by Conrail. *Mike Harting*

By the Conrail era, though anthracite was no longer a dominant source of railroad traffic or profits, a number of anthracite mines continued to generate carloads of coal. In this July 29, 1992, view of the Reading & Northern, Conrail hopper 489989 is part of a loaded train coming down a new connection at Lofty, Pennsylvania. *Mike Harting*

Reading and CNJ provided a through route between Philadelphia and the New York metro area, as well as through routes between New York and Harrisburg and Williamsport.

Reading also had ties with the Lehigh Valley Railroad, and for many years the Lehigh Valley provided Reading with a westward gateway to Buffalo, while Reading moved Lehigh Valley traffic to Philadelphia.

In 1913, Reading carried 12.8 million tons of anthracite, giving it the largest share of the Pennsylvania anthracite market. Although volumes declined precipitously in the mid-twentieth century, Reading remained the region's largest anthracite hauler. When it was melded into Conrail in 1976, Reading was one of the few traditional anthracite lines still moving any volume of hard coal. Today, portions of the old Reading are operated by the

Conrail-era spinoff short line Reading & Northern, which continues to earn a significant portion of its income as an anthracite hauler.

IN 1913, READING CARRIED 12.8 MILLION TONS OF ANTHRACITE, GIVING IT THE LARGEST SHARE OF THE PENNSYLVANIA MARKET.

Lehigh Valley Railroad

In 1851, coal magnate Asa Packer took control of the company that he soon renamed Lehigh Valley Railroad and developed into an anthracite empire. The railroad expanded in the second half of the nineteenth century, pushing its line through the Lehigh

Right: One of Lehigh Valley's 4-8-4 Wyoming types leads an anthracite train. In the mid-1930s, when locomotive building ebbed as a result of difficult economic times, Lehigh Valley bucked the trend and bought new high-output 4-8-4s, dividing its order between Alco and Baldwin. *Railroad Museum of Pennsylvania PHMC*

Below: A pair of Conrail MP15s and an SW1500 spot empties at the Gilberton coal breaker at Locust Summit, Pennsylvania, in September 1995. *Mike Harting*

Gorge and into the coalfields of the Wyoming Valley over Penobscot Mountain. Ultimately it built a line east across New Jersey to the shore of the Hudson at Jersey City opposite Manhattan. By 1892, LV had built west to Buffalo, New York—a crucial gateway for interchanging coal and merchandise traffic.

By 1899, Lehigh Valley was moving more than 11.3 million tons of coal annually. LV's anthracite traffic declined during the twentieth century, like the traffic of its neighbors in eastern Pennsylvania. Though LV continued to use the black diamond as its logo, by the time it was merged into Conrail in 1976, its anthracite traffic was insignificant.

Delaware, Lackawanna & Western

Conceived in the late 1840s as a broad gauge feeder to the Erie Railroad, the Delaware, Lackawanna & Western began in Scranton, the heart of northern anthracite territory, and gradually extended its main line to reach coal markets. It built east over the Poconos and through the Delaware Water Gap to New Jersey. Initially, it relied on a connection with

Central Railroad of New Jersey to forward its traffic toward New York City but later completed its own all-rail route to the Hudson shore at Hoboken. Like the Lehigh Valley, DL&W built north and west into New York state, ultimately reaching Buffalo. Secondary lines to Utica, Ithaca, Syracuse, and the Lake Ontario port at Oswego were driven by the desire to tap anthracite markets, while lines in Pennsylvania furthered its penetration of the anthracite fields. Most important among these was the Lackawanna & Bloomsburg line (melded into DL&W in the 1870s), which served as a significant anthracite gathering line while giving the railroad a strategic connection with the Reading Company and Pennsylvania Railroad at Sunbury.

When William H. Truesdale assumed control of the railroad in 1899, DL&W was moving about 6.3 million tons annually. Through skillful management and massive capital improvement, Truesdale transformed DL&W's infrastructure into a super railroad and simultaneously advanced its anthracite business. His engineers re-profiled Lackawanna's mountain

Anthracite was the lifeblood of the DL&W. Under William Truesdale, the railroad's main line was expanded to three-track on the grade east of Scranton toward Pocono Summit to better accommodate a mix of coal, merchandise, and passenger traffic. In this 1913 photograph, three 2-8-0s—one on the front, two at the back—labor with 25 cars of coal east of Scranton along Roaring Brook. *T. T. Taber collection, Railroad Museum of Pennsylvania PHMC*

25

This 1883 glass-plate photograph shows DL&W's extensive anthracite storage docks at Port Morris, New Jersey. This site developed in the mid-nineteenth century because it was where the railroad fed the Morris Canal that connected the Delaware River at a point near Phillipsburg with the Hudson River at Jersey City. Although the transfer to canal boats waned as the DL&W grew in importance, Port Morris developed as a seasonal coal-storage facility. *T. T. Taber collection, Railroad Museum of Pennsylvania PHMC*

main lines by relocating alignments to lower maximum gradients and minimizing curvature. This improved efficiency, increased capacity, and lowered operating expenses, thus enabling the DL&W to haul more coal traffic and better accommodate merchandise and passenger business. By the time the antitrust Hepburn Act that ultimately separated railroads from mining companies was passed in 1906, DL&W had nearly doubled its anthracite tonnage.

The DL&W gathered coal from more than 40 mines in the Scranton area and along branches in the region, especially the Hanover & Newport line and the Bloomsburg Division. Coal cars were assembled

into trains at various Scranton-area yards; originally work was done in downtown Scranton, but as the volume of coal grew, DL&W built large new yards, first at Taylor and then at Hampton in 1911. In the 1910s and 1920s, DL&W originated as many as 1,000 loaded hoppers daily from Scranton.

Eastward trains faced a 1.50 ruling grade over Pocono Summit. In the 1920s, typical DL&W coal trains consisted of 40 to 50 cars and required two 2-8-0 Consolidation-type locomotives on the head end with another three in rear-end helper service. As trains made eastward progress, helper engines were cut off and returned downgrade. West of Scranton, the main line climbed over Clarks Summit, where the ruling grade was 0.63 percent after construction of the Summit Cutoff in 1915 reduced the grade by 0.55 percent.

As DL&W matured, it expanded and refined its coal terminals. At Port Morris, New Jersey, the railroad had an early facility where it transferred coal to the Morris Canal. Later this developed as a seasonal coal-storage facility and ultimately became one of the railroad's most important yards. At Hoboken, the

DL&W's extensive elevated Pier 5 at Hoboken used both steam and electrically powered car dumpers to unload coal into marine vessels for local delivery in New York Harbor and beyond. It is pictured in the early twentieth century with a coastal barge. *T. T. Taber collection, Railroad Museum of Pennsylvania PHMC*

The Morris Canal developed as a coal corridor in the 1830s, a generation before the DL&W. This photo, dated about 1870, shows Port Morris in its role as a seasonal coal-storage facility. In later years Port Morris was one of DL&W's more important freight yards. It was closed in the Erie Lackawanna era, long after anthracite had faded as the primary traffic on the line. *T. T. Taber collection, Railroad Museum of Pennsylvania PHMC*

railroad built extensive yards and waterfront facilities on the banks of the Hudson opposite Manhattan. DL&W's Pier 5 at Hoboken was an extensive elevated facility where car dumpers transloaded anthracite into marine vessels for local delivery.

DL&W operated a seasonal Lake Ontario port facility at Oswego. Authors Thomas T. Taber and Thomas T. Taber III detail this and other facilities in their three-volume work on the Lackawanna. In 1882, DL&W replaced its early dockside facilities at Oswego with an impressive 480-foot coal trestle featuring a side-pocket arrangement for loading lake ships. This facility operated for more than five decades; at peak times it handled up to 2,000 tons daily. In its best years, an estimated 400,000 tons of

This September 19, 1929, view of DL&W's Pier 5 at Hoboken was exposed using an 8x10-inch camera. The pier was 1,283 feet long, and mechanized facilities were built here in 1903 to augment older facilities at Pier 10 that dated from the 1880s. *T. T. Taber collection, Railroad Museum of Pennsylvania PHMC*

At Hoboken, DL&W transloaded great volumes of coal from freight cars to marine vessels. In this view a car has its contents dumped into a chute that directs the coal to a waiting boat below. In his 1912 book *Freight Terminals and Trains*, John A. Droege notes that this facility was specially built for anthracite and could handle up to 30 cars an hour. *T. T. Taber collection, Railroad Museum of Pennsylvania PHMC*

coal were transferred to ships. In 1935, the old trestle was replaced with a modern coal dumper. As its volume of anthracite declined, DL&W began handling bituminous coal from off-line sources. Following the opening of the St. Lawrence Seaway in 1959, the Oswego facilities couldn't accommodate the largest lake boats, so they closed in 1963.

Among DL&W's most important coal-transfer facilities were those at Buffalo, where it interchanged with other carriers and transloaded coal into lake boats for shipment across Lake Erie. In 1882 it had constructed the lakeside North Pier coal docks, and by the 1890s it had built a massive coal-storage trestle in East Buffalo. Expanded during 1916, the North Pier was capable of moving 7,000 tons daily, with annual coal transfer of up to 1.5 million tons (during the six months when Lake Erie was open to navigation).

DL&W's locomotives were largely anthracite burners, and its typical heavy-freight locomotive of the 1910 period was a 2-8-0 camelback with a large, shallow firebox grate designed to burn anthracite waste—commonly known as culm. At its peak, DL&W's locomotives consumed as much as 1.5 million tons of anthracite annually. DL&W, like most of the other anthracite lines, moved toward bituminous-burning locomotives after World War I.

During the 1920s, in an effort to improve speed and efficiency, DL&W bought three-cylinder Mountain–type locomotives designed for heavy drag service. Taber indicates that a pair of three-cylinder Mountain types, with a pair of 2-8-0s shoving at the back, could lift 80 cars of coal weighing an estimated 4,000 tons east from Scranton up to Nay Aug.

The DL&W continued to move large volumes of anthracite through the late 1920s, but volume tapered off over the next three decades. By the early 1950s, DL&W had augmented declining anthracite business with bridge traffic and bituminous coal interchanged with other carriers. When DL&W and the Erie Railroad merged in 1960 to form the Erie Lackawanna, the movement of anthracite was only a fraction of what it had been just a few decades earlier.

Erie Railroad

Broad gauge Erie (until 1878, Erie's rails were 6 feet apart, compared with 4 feet 8.5 inches on most lines) penetrated anthracite country by building and acquiring lines into the Wyoming Valley. Its Wyoming Division comprised the old Erie & Wyoming Valley Railroad, reaching southwest from its main line at Lackawaxen and running to Dunmore (near Scranton) and Pittston. Its Jefferson Division cut compass south from the junction at the west end of its famous Starrucca Viaduct (near at Lanesboro), crossing Ararat Summit to reach Carbondale and Scranton. Erie shared the latter route with the Delaware & Hudson, which used it to reach its own main line at Nineveh, New York.

Unlike most anthracite roads that were largely focused on coal movement, Erie was built to carry east–west traffic; not only did it connect with

The anthracite railroads typically used a variety of slow-burning slack anthracite coal known as culm, which required a wider, shallower firebox than used for other fuels. This Erie & Wyoming Valley Railroad camelback features a Wootten firebox developed by the general manager of the Philadelphia & Reading, John E. Wootten, in the 1870s. The Erie & Wyoming Valley was leased by the Erie Railroad and later operated as its Wyoming Division. *W. A. Lucas collection, Railroad Museum of Pennsylvania PHMC*

Great Lakes ports—first at Dunkirk and later at Buffalo—but ultimately reached Chicago, America's foremost railroad gateway. Likewise, its coal ambitions were not limited to hauling anthracite, since it later extended several lines into the northern bituminous fields in central and western Pennsylvania. Here, in addition to its own trackage, it shared trackage with the New York Central, the Buffalo, Rochester & Pittsburgh, and the Pennsylvania Railroad.

In 1906, the Erie Railroad ordered 6,000 coal hoppers in the series 25000–30999; its affiliated New York, Susquehanna & Western ordered another 300 cars of a similar design numbered 8000–8299. All were built by Standard Steel Car Company. Erie hopper 26589 is shown in 1923 after being retrofitted with safety appliances to comply with the U.S. Safety Appliances Act. *T. T. Taber collection, Railroad Museum of Pennsylvania PHMC*

New York, Ontario & Western

Commonly referred to as the O&W, this railroad began in 1866 as the New York & Oswego Midland, which aimed to connect its namesake points by way of the Catskills. Completed from the west shore of the Hudson to the Lake Ontario port of Oswego in 1873, the railroad was in financial difficulty from the start and was reorganized as the New York, Ontario & Western in 1879. In 1890, O&W built a 55-mile branch from its main line at Cadosia, New York, to Wyoming Valley anthracite fields at Scranton.

As a latecomer to the region—it was one of eight steam railroads to serve the area—O&W had one of the most difficult lines into this lucrative coal-producing center, yet mine products fueled the railroad's coffers for the better part of 50 years. To accommodate substantially heavier trains needed to haul coal, O&W extensively upgraded its lines east of the coalfields, which required rebuilding bridges and laying heavier rail.

During the first decade of the twentieth century, coal traffic was sufficiently robust for the railroad to install directional double-track on most of its Scranton Division and on the main line east from Cadosia to its connection with New York Central's West Shore route (allowing the railroad access to Weehawken, New Jersey, opposite Manhattan).

O&W's coal operations were based at Mayfield Yard, located a few miles north of Scranton, not far from Delaware & Hudson's extensive coal yards. It built substantial coal piers at Oswego and Cornwall, New York (on the Hudson), and later at West New York, near Weehawken, New Jersey. Its Oswego pier was located across the river from Delaware, Lackawanna &

Western's facilities. At Cornwall, the railroad operated a pair of tugs to deliver coal barges to customers in the lower Hudson Valley. O&W's West New York Coal Piers 1 and 2 were profiled in the *1955 Keystone Coal Buyers Manual*. These dual piers had 650-foot outside berths and a 400-foot slip between them and could easily load two ships simultaneously. Two electric telescopic chutes were used for loading vessels. In later years the piers loaded bituminous coal and coke, as well as anthracite, and were capable of handling 500,000 tons per year. A storage yard had track space for 200 loaded cars and 150 empties.

In 1904, New Haven Railroad took control of O&W, an action coincident with its move to control the Central New England and thus circumvent Pennsylvania Railroad's high tariffs for traffic (especially anthracite) moving through New York City. Using CNE's Poughkeepsie Bridge route, O&W's anthracite flowed via the Maybrook gateway to the vibrant New England market.

The stiff grades east of Mayfield required helpers. Here, O&W assigned its famous X-class 2-10-2s, known colloquially as Bull Moose locomotives. Despite general declines in the anthracite industry after World War I, O&W's business remained strong and peaked in 1932. Author William F. Helmer, in his book *O&W: The Long Life and Slow Death of the New York, Ontario and Western Railway*, points out that as late as the early 1930s, anthracite represented roughly 70 percent of the railroad's freight tonnage.

Next page: On September 31, 1937, New York, Ontario & Western Class Y 4-8-2 No. 408 and Class U-1 camelback No. 244 lead a coal train at Dumont, New Jersey. *Railroad Museum of Pennsylvania PHMC*

Yet, as important as this was for O&W, it was just a trickle compared with the tide of anthracite moving to consumer markets from eastern Pennsylvania. Robert E. Mohowski, author of *New York, Ontario & Western in the Diesel Age*, writes that O&W anthracite traffic in the early 1930s was just 4 percent of that in Pennsylvania.

In 1937, the bottom fell out of the anthracite market, causing several mines affiliated with the O&W to fail. The railroad sought reorganization, but it was the beginning of the end. The railroad shut its Oswego pier in 1938. Under the administration of a receiver, the railroad struggled along for another two decades. Its traffic peaked again during World War II, but by the time the railroad was abandoned in 1957, it was moving very little coal.

Central Railroad of New Jersey

In its early days, Central Railroad of New Jersey served as a bridge route for coal moving over the Lehigh Valley and Delaware, Lackawanna & Western railroads to the New York/New Jersey waterfront. This changed in the 1870s, when both LV and DL&W pushed their own lines east to the Hudson River. CNJ reacted, extending its influence west into anthracite country by leasing the recently completed Lehigh & Susquehanna from the anthracite pioneer Lehigh Coal & Navigation Company. With this acquisition CNJ reached White Haven via Mauch Chunk and from there ultimately extended its main line northwest to Scranton. Not only was much of CNJ's line parallel to Lehigh Valley, but in many places their main lines ran side by side. CNJ's expansion not only secured the railroad a good portion of anthracite traffic but also enabled it to acquire coal lands and mines as well, a move consistent with the trend set by other railroads in the region.

IN 1926, CNJ HAULED 1,154,333 COAL CARS—MUCH OF IT ANTHRACITE.

Among the more unusual aspects of CNJ's operation were the Ashley Planes, built by the Lehigh & Susquehanna in 1843 to connect the Lehigh Canal with the north branch division of the Pennsylvania Canal at Wilkes-Barre. This was among the last inclined railways in heavy freight service and survived until 1948 when it was replaced by a circuitous conventional railroad line.

While not the busiest anthracite line, CNJ's coal traffic was substantial: in 1926, it hauled 1,154,333 cars—much of it anthracite.

The Rise and Fall of Anthracite Empires

In 1840, anthracite production had reached 864,000 tons annually; by 1860 this had increased nearly tenfold to 8.5 million tons. Following the Civil War, legal changes enabled railroads to make substantial acquisitions of coal-bearing land and mining companies. As a result, anthracite railroads became involved in the businesses of both mining and transporting coal. By 1867, annual anthracite production had crested 13 million tons and was rising rapidly. The majority of anthracite-producing land was bought by the various anthracite-hauling railroads in just a few years. In 1902, 96 percent of the anthracite fields were owned by railroads, with the Reading Company controlling the largest share.

Perceptions of greed and gross mismanagement, combined with compulsive overbuilding by railroads nationwide, sparked occasional tremors that appeared to threaten the economic fabric. As the public became weary of perceived railroad abuses, legislation was drafted to curb railroad profits and level the playing field. The Hepburn Act of 1906 forced railroads to divest themselves of coal properties and mines and allowed the Interstate Commerce Commission to set maximum railroad shipping rates. These new laws coincided with

IN 1902, 96 PERCENT OF EASTERN ANTHRACITE FIELDS WERE OWNED BY RAILROADS.

new market challenges to the anthracite lines, such as growing highway competition that had begun to siphon away non-coal traffic, and a series of bitter strikes between miners and mine owners resulted in work stoppages—sometimes lasting for months—that encouraged homeowners to adopt other heating fuels. After World War I, the demand for anthracite as a home-heating fuel waned. As noted earlier, even most of the anthracite railroads switched to bituminous-burning locomotives. Yet all of these changes occurred over several years. Despite a loss of market share, demand for anthracite remained robust into the 1920s, spurred by the growth of the post–World War I American economy.

Anthracite's more precipitous decline in the middle years of the twentieth century seemed to exemplify the poor condition of American railroads. Many lines closely tied to anthracite were incapable of adequately replacing it with other types of traffic and suffered terribly as a result. The once busy lines became rusty reminders of another era. The first noteworthy carrier to fold was Erie Railroad affiliate Wilkes-Barre & Eastern, abandoned in 1939. By the mid-1950s, with redundant lines lacing the region, carriers considered consolidation. Others were liquidated, notably the New York, Ontario & Western in 1957.

By the time of the Conrail bailout in 1976 (see Chapter 3), which included most of the surviving former anthracite lines—Erie Lackawanna, Lehigh Valley, Central Railroad of New Jersey, Reading, and Lehigh & Hudson River—anthracite hauling was nearly irrelevant as a source of traffic.

Putting figures to this change, the *1955 Keystone Coal Buyers Manual* reported there were still 73 mining companies in eastern Pennsylvania working 87 sources of hard coal and that total anthracite tonnage mined was 30,495,391 tons. Mining output slipped steadily, and 20 years later the total annual anthracite tonnage was only 5,875,000 tons. The figure bottomed out in the 1980s and started to rebound nominally in the early 1990s.

Key to Conrail's survival strategy was rationalization of its physical plant. During its 24-year reign, it downgraded, abandoned, or sold much of the infrastructure that had been developed to move anthracite. By the late 1990s many of the railway lines that had served the anthracite region were either gone or reduced to weedy, slow-speed, stub-end branches.

Most of Conrail's remaining anthracite-region trackage was conveyed to Norfolk Southern when the railroad was divided between NS and CSX in 1998–1999. Today it is difficult to imagine the vast, intensive, and complex bustling enterprises involved in the transport of Pennsylvania anthracite. Rights of way have been reclaimed by nature, and the odd rusty bridge, cinder-lined track bed, looming slag heap, and crumbling ruins of old coal breakers are the only hints of the business that once dominated the economy and the landscape.

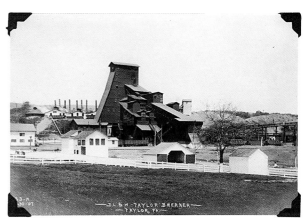

Above: DL&W's Taylor Breaker opened in 1868 and operated for approximately 90 years. This photo dates from 1907. The facility was upgraded in 1910, at which time it was producing an average of 1,440 tons daily. It was located on the Taylor Branch in Scranton, just a short distance from the railroad's massive Taylor Yard. *T. T. Taber collection, Railroad Museum of Pennsylvania PHMC*

Left: A Conrail coal hopper on the coal dumper at Pier 24 in Philadelphia on August 13, 1991. Several anthracite coal companies on Conrail supplied coal to Quebec Iron & Titanium for use in separating titanium from iron in the unprocessed ore they mined. Coal going to QI&T was blended for use in their industrial process. In 1992 anthracite traffic that had moved through Pier 24 was shifted to the CONSOL Energy Terminal in Baltimore. *Mike Harting*

Chapter 2 HISTORICAL
APPALACHIAN BITUMINOUS COAL

This C&O publicity photo depicts brand-new H-8 2-6-6-6 Allegheny No. 1654 leading a westbound empty coal train up the 1.14 percent ruling grade at Moss Run toward Alleghany Summit. This was one of 20 Alleghenies built for C&O by Lima in 1948. The different spellings of Alleghany have caused a great deal of confusion. The locomotive was named the Allegheny type (with an "e") because C&O and Lima folks were from Cleveland where the spelling was standard. Alleghany (with an "a") is a local Virginia spelling also used by C&O for its mainline summit. *C&O photo, Jay Williams collection*

The bituminous coalfields of Appalachia are among the richest carbon energy sources on the planet and have been viewed as a potential source of railroad traffic from an early date. In the formative years of railroading, eastern Pennsylvania anthracite fields dominated home-heating markets and early industrial enterprise, with the commercial development of bituminous coalfields following closely. The iron industry around Pittsburgh and the city's home-heating demand provided two of the first significant commercial markets for bituminous coal. Shyamal K. Majumdar and E. Willard Miller, in their book *Pennsylvania Coal: Resources, Technology, and Utilization*, note that by the mid-nineteenth century Pittsburgh was consuming 400,000 tons annually for home-heating alone. The Pittsburgh bituminous market and related transport on the Ohio River fed railroads, especially the Pennsylvania Railroad, in the years prior to the Civil War.

Bituminous coal really came into its own after the Civil War, when a flurry of railroad construction in central Pennsylvania tapped rich bituminous fields. Railroads affiliated with the New York Central, Pennsylvania Railroad, and Erie Railroad vied with smaller companies for both territory and traffic, mimicking the duplicative networks that had developed in anthracite country.

During the 1870s and 1880s, rapid development of coalfields in West Virginia, southern Ohio, and eastern Kentucky encouraged penetration of these mountainous areas by new railroads, notably Norfolk & Western and Chesapeake & Ohio, while enriching established lines like the Baltimore & Ohio and Louisville & Nashville. By 1899, the swell of bituminous coal traffic allowed the United States to surpass Britain as the world's leading coal producer. The flow of bituminous enriched the railroads that carried it and gradually edged out anthracite as the most significant source of railroad traffic.

Baltimore & Ohio

The Baltimore & Ohio was chartered on February 28, 1827, to build from the port city of Baltimore,

The Cranberry Grade was the most significant challenge to the B&O. Not only was it the steepest multiple-track main line east of the Rockies, it also was an exceptionally sinuous ascent of the "Alleghanies" (as spelled by B&O on its West End). At Salt Lick Curve at 11:25 a.m. on June 12, 1949, two Baldwin Class EL2 2-8-8-0s work the back of a 50-car train, while another two pull hard at the head end. Built in 1916, these were originally Mallet compounds but were converted to simple operation after 1927. *Bruce Fales, Jay Williams collection*

Maryland, to the Ohio River. It was slow to reach this goal, and by 1842, B&O had reached only as far west as Cumberland, Maryland. Farther west the railroad faced stiff mountain grades and expensive construction. Fortunately, coal deposits around Cumberland provided a lucrative source of traffic that soon developed into B&O's predominant business. In *History of the Baltimore & Ohio*,

BY 1848, COAL REPRESENTED 60 PERCENT OF B&O'S EASTBOUND FREIGHT, ACCOUNTING FOR 60,000 TONS ANNUALLY.

John F. Stover traces the railroad's growth and cites many relevant traffic figures. By 1848, for example, coal represented 60 percent of B&O's eastbound freight traffic and accounted for 60,000 tons annually. Over the years the tide of coal would sweep the railroad. In 1849, B&O established a coal dock at Locust Point in Baltimore. In 1850, it moved 132,000 tons.

Climbing over the spine of the Alleghenies, the railroad engineered its famous grades that defined operations west of Cumberland for more than a century. This portion of the B&O became known as the West End. B&O finally reached the Ohio River at Wheeling, Virginia (later West Virginia), in 1852. Over the years B&O's Benwood Yard south of Wheeling emerged as an important location for its coal operations. A second line to

Above: On September 25, 1955, a Baltimore & Ohio Mikado switches coal cars at the yards that fed the Lake Erie coal docks at Fairport, Ohio. B&O, like other Appalachian bituminous haulers, moved a considerable tonnage of coal northwest to the Great Lakes for transloading to boats. *Jim Shaughnessy*

Left: Narrow gauge mine cars of raw coal are loaded at the Shannopin Mine in Bobtown, Pennsylvania, on October 2, 1990. The coal was moved to a car dumper then loaded into standard gauge hopper cars for shipment via the Monongahela Railway. *Mike Harting*

the Ohio River, known as the Parkersburg Branch, was built due west to its namesake city downriver from Wheeling.

Located at the eastern edge of one of the most productive coalfields in Appalachia, Grafton, West Virginia, was developed as a significant marshaling point for B&O's coal trains. In addition to the extensive yards and locomotive facilities built here, Grafton served as the offices of the Monongah Division.

On B&O's Lake Branch on August 27, 1955, EM1 2-8-8-4 No. 7611 waits at Fales Spur (south of Painesville, Ohio) for a loaded coal train led by another EM1 to pull forward. No. 7611 will tie on the back of the heavy train to work as a pusher over the remaining miles to B&O's Lake Erie coal docks at Fairport Harbor. *Jim Shaughnessy*

B&O carried 452,000 tons in 1855, and by 1884 coal traffic swelled to 2.8 million tons. In the 1890s, B&O aggressively expanded its operations in West Virginia and southern Ohio coalfields by building and acquiring key routes that enabled it to increase its coal business dramatically. During the twentieth century the Monongah Division originated the lion's share of B&O-hauled coal.

Much of B&O-hauled coal was sent east over the West End. Loaded trains first climbed the Newburg Grade, cresting at Tunnelton, West Virginia, then dropped down the Cheat River Grade, only to climb the brutal Cranberry Grade, one of the steepest prolonged mainline grades east of the Rockies. Topping out at Terra Alta, West Virginia, trains then had to descend the legendary Seventeen Mile Grade between the summit of the Alleghenies at Altamont, Maryland, and Keyser, West Virginia. So feared was this long and steep descent that B&O installed two runaway tracks.

To better facilitate the movement of eastward coal traffic, in 1900 B&O built the Paterson Creek Cutoff east of the West End grades, enabling coal trains to bypass the sprawling yards at Cumberland while providing a more direct and substantially shorter route east. In conjunction with this new line,

A southward Baltimore & Ohio freight moves coal empties and merchandise traffic on the former Buffalo, Rochester & Pittsburgh at Lewis Run, south of Bradford, Pennsylvania, in the late 1940s. No. 7583 is a former BR&P Mallet compound typical of the railroad in later steam years. *Gordon Roth*

B&O built a large coal yard at Keyser to handle West End coal traffic. At that time, B&O boasted a fleet of 28,000 coal cars.

By 1910, the railroad was handling 23 million tons annually, and the volume would continue to climb. In 1948, B&O carried nearly 42 million tons. In addition to coal destined for Locust Point, B&O interchanged eastward coal with other railroads, while some coal moved via B&O's trackage rights over the Reading and the Central Railroad of New Jersey to B&O's coal docks at Staten Island. This facility allowed B&O to compete in the busy New York City market. Traditionally, B&O served docks at St. George on Staten Island, but after World War II these were replaced with high-volume facilities at Howland Hook. S. Kip Farrington Jr. reports in *Railroading the Modern Way* that this latter facility could accommodate up to 128 carloads of coal every eight hours. B&O also shipped coal northwest from West Virginia mines to the Great Lakes ports, and west to Cincinnati.

B&O's vision of a low-grade, east–west main line across central Pennsylvania, with a routing shorter than the original B&O main line between New York and Chicago, resulted in B&O's acquisition of the Buffalo, Rochester & Pittsburgh and Buffalo & Susquehanna railroads in the early 1930s. These acquisitions conveniently coincided with federal efforts at planned railroad consolidation, which aided B&O by rapid ICC approval.

Both regional railroads happened to serve coalfields in north-central Pennsylvania and contributed to B&O's coal haulage, even though they weren't acquired by the larger railroad to haul coal. The BR&P was by far the more significant of the two. It had been built as a coal conduit in the 1880s and served coalfields in the vicinity of Dubois and

Punxsutawney using a network of branches. It also vied for territory and traffic with New York Central's affiliates, as well as the Pennsylvania and Erie railroads and smaller lines.

BR&P's main line connected its namesake cities and B&O's Fourth Subdivision, which ran north to Rochester, New York (and beyond to a coal port at Charlotte, located at the mouth of the Genesee River at Lake Ontario), and carried the largest volume of coal. BR&P began shipping via Charlotte in the 1880s, and in 1909 it expanded capacity there with a high-volume coal trestle. This facility was substantially expanded in 1913, by which time the BR&P was handling upward of 1 million tons of bituminous coal annually at this outlet. In addition the railroad shipped whole coal cars from Charlotte to Canadian customers via a Lake Ontario car ferry, while coal for eastern markets was interchanged with the Erie, Lehigh Valley, Delaware, Lackawanna & Western, and New York Central (via its West Shore lines).

As West Virginia markets expanded after World War I, BR&P's coal market declined. By the time B&O bought the line, its best coal-hauling days were behind it. Yet the Charlotte docks remained active until the late 1960s, and the line hosted unit trains for Kodak at Rochester into the late 1980s. Under CSX, most of the BR&P route was sold to Genesee & Wyoming's Rochester & Southern (1986) and Buffalo & Pittsburgh (1988). In 2008, Buffalo & Pittsburgh continued to move a healthy volume of coal from four on-line Pennsylvania mines.

Western Maryland

In 1902, George Gould took control of the Western Maryland as part of a scheme to string together a transcontinental railroad network. With a mix of new construction and line acquisition, he extended the WM to Cumberland and beyond into the coalfields of West Virginia.

Gould also set into motion construction of WM's Connellsville, Pennsylvania, extension. Although Gould failed to achieve his transcontinental ambitions, WM was transformed into an Appalachian bituminous carrier. Among Gould's improvements were construction of the Western Maryland Tidewater Railroad Company and the Port Covington coal pier at Baltimore. After modernization in 1930, the Port Covington dumper was able to accommodate one loaded car per minute, giving WM ample transloading capacity.

WM served bituminous mines in western Maryland, Pennsylvania, and, most importantly, West Virginia. It forwarded coal east on its Bergoo and Elkins lines, both of which featured long sections of 3 percent grades requiring substantial use of helpers—the heaviest trains would feature as many as 10 2-8-0 Consolidation-type locomotives spaced among the coal cars. Once over the mountains, coal was dispatched east from yards at Cumberland and Hagerstown.

Coal was also forwarded north–northeast from Hagerstown to the New York, Philadelphia, and New England markets via a connection with the Reading at Lurgan, Pennsylvania. E. L. Thompson, writing in Frank P. Donovan's *Railroads of America* in 1948, states that approximately 50 percent of WM freight tonnage came from coal haulage, while noting that coal reserves along WM lines had been estimated at 4 billion tons.

Much of the WM was directly parallel with the Baltimore & Ohio. Although the WM was managed independently for many years, it was gradually absorbed by the Chesapeake & Ohio–controlled Chessie System from the late 1960s to the early 1980s. Much of WM's trackage was abandoned in favor of B&O trackage (also absorbed into the Chessie System), although WM coal feeders have continued to produce tonnage for Chessie System's corporate successor, CSX, to the present day.

SOME OF THE HEAVIEST WM BITUMINOUS TRAINS FEATURED AS MANY AS 10 2-8-0 CONSOLIDATION TYPES SPACED AMONG THE CARS.

Chesapeake & Ohio

The Chesapeake & Ohio (C&O) was formed in 1868 by the merger of the Virginia Central and the Covington & Ohio. During the 1870s, under the administration of Collis P. Huntington, C&O expanded rapidly. By April 1873, the railroad had 428 route miles that reached from Richmond to the new Ohio River town named Huntington, West Virginia. Additional feeders were extended into the coal-rich area of central Appalachia—colorfully described as the "Coal Bin." Through connecting lines, C&O reached Cincinnati in 1881. In 1882, C&O completed a strategic route east from Richmond to the tidewater port of Newport News, Virginia, which rapidly developed as a primary coal conduit. Although C&O's finances faltered under Huntington's administration, in 1888 Vanderbilt interests backed by Drexel, Morgan & Company assumed control.

At Alleghany Summit, Virginia, on October 7, 1947, massive C&O Class H-8 Allegheny No. 1618 works as a pusher at the back of a 116-car coal train. Because of its close ties to coal, C&O continued to order big steam after World War II when most railroads were ordering large numbers of new diesels. Lima built 60 of these powerful 2-6-6-6 locomotives for C&O between 1941 and 1948. *Bruce D. Fales, Jay Williams collection*

With adequate financing, the railroad continued to expand, opening a variety of additional routes.

Using the low-grade Richmond & Alleghany railroad, C&O opened a superior route for coal bound for Newport News. C&O also secured trackage rights over the Southern Railway route to Washington, D.C. By the turn of the twentieth century, C&O had assembled an enviable network reaching from the tidewater, through the heart of one of the richest bituminous coal-producing areas in the world, and on to key gateways at Cincinnati and Columbus.

The steps of C&O's JD Tower at Clifton Forge made for a good vantage point to view this eastbound coal train on May 11, 1947. C&O's K-3 Mikado is working hard with 160 loads in tow as it heads toward Newport News.
Bruce D. Fales, Jay Williams collection

Coal accounted for roughly 50 percent of its traffic and revenue.

In 1903, C&O bought part ownership of the Hocking Valley Railroad, a strategic line that reached from the Ohio River port of Galipolis, Ohio, to Toledo on the shore of Lake Erie. To better link to this line, C&O built a route called C&O Northern. In 1910 it further cemented its western connections with the acquisition of the Chicago, Cincinnati & Louisville to provide a direct link to Chicago. Despite its strategic Chicago connection, C&O's Hocking Valley route proved the more valuable coal corridor.

In 1923, the Van Sweringen brothers, Oris P. and Mantis J., bought control of the C&O. By the early 1930s they had assembled a railroad empire that included the Pere Marquette, Erie Railroad, Wheeling & Lake Erie, Missouri Pacific, and Chicago & Eastern Illinois. In the 1930s, C&O benefited from access to capital that allowed substantial modernization and capacity improvement. However, financial distress brought on by the Great Depression ultimately unraveled the Van Sweringen empire, and during 1935 and 1936, financial wizard Robert Young took control; in 1942, he became chairman of C&O and in 1947 merged C&O and Pere Marquette. By this time C&O had emerged as one of America's foremost coal haulers. Young went on to run New York Central in the 1950s.

In *Railroads at War*, respected railroad author S. Kip Farrington Jr. offers a detailed profile of

C&O's coal operations at the height of World War II, when the railroad was gushing rivers of coal over its main lines. In 1943, C&O operated 3,092 route miles—1,708 of main line and 1,384 of branch line. Of the latter, more than 1,000 miles laced the coalfields in southern West Virginia, eastern Kentucky, and southern Ohio, which composed the heart of C&O's empire. There, it served four distinct coal districts that produced 62.6 million tons of bituminous annually (C&O carried an additional 15 million tons of coal from interchanges with other lines for a total of 77.7 million tons in 1943). Of the Hocking, Kanawha, Kentucky, and New River districts, Kanawha was the oldest and by far the most productive. Coal was mined there as early 1817, and in 1943 it originated 27.3 million tons for C&O. Next in volume was the New River District, with 12.75 million tons.

Two Chesapeake & Ohio F7As lead a loaded coal train through Covington, Kentucky, on July 28, 1958. The two locomotives provided just 3,000 horsepower. Immediately behind the locomotives is a pair of loaded outside-braced, drop-bottom gondolas lettered for Louisville & Nashville. *Richard Jay Solomon*

A considerable volume of coal flowed eastward to Newport News, where C&O operated massive port facilities on the north side of the Hampton Roads estuary opposite Norfolk, Virginia. Coal was by far the most important commodity moved through Newport News, but it was not the only traffic handled here, and Farrington points out that C&O's port was the largest terminal of its kind operated by a single railroad. In 1943, for 24 hours a day, two enormous coal piers, Nos. 9 and 15, poured coal from hoppers to waiting ships and barges. Keeping traffic flowing to the docks was a never-ending parade of trains from

This was a vision of modern railroading—Chesapeake & Ohio style. On October 7, 1947, C&O Allegheny No. 1644 leads 88 empty hoppers past Alleghany, Virginia. C&O's Allegheny steam locomotives used a 2-6-6-6 wheel arrangement and were among the heaviest ever built, weighing even more than Union Pacific's massive Big Boys. *Bruce D. Fales, Jay Williams collection*

the coalfields. C&O's massive classification yards at Clifton Forge sent 160-car trains east to Newport News. On arrival, they were staged in 1 of 10 receiving tracks, each long enough to accommodate an entire train. Coal cars ready for dumping were positioned on 1 of 35 tracks that fed the piers. In addition, C&O maintained Dawson City Yards, which had storage capacity for 3,500 cars. Farrington writes than in 1942, Newport News transferred 4,283,000 tons of coal from rail to water. During the war, some C&O-shipped coal destined for New York, New England, and elsewhere on the Atlantic seaboard was sent over less efficient all-rail routes because of the threat posed by German submarines.

Like its primary competitor, Norfolk & Western, C&O shipped more coal west than east. At Huntington, West Virginia, the railroad served a large transfer facility on the Ohio River where three companies operated tipples that delivered coal to barges. At peak times during the war, C&O dumped as many as 219 cars a day and, on average, 331,786 tons a month. In 1943, this totaled more than 3.9 million tons.

Westbound coal gathered from multiple mines on C&O's branches and along its main line between Hawks Nest and Meadow Creek, West Virginia, was weighed and classified at a specially built hump yard at Russell, Kentucky. This facility dated from 1918 and was significantly improved nine years later with the installation of car retarders. By 1943 it was one of the largest yards in the country and could handle more than 14,000 cars daily. Trains departed daily to key gateways. Some traffic was interchanged with the Pennsylvania Railroad at Columbus. Other trains continued to Cincinnati.

C&O also interchanged trains with the Erie Railroad at Marion, Ohio, and with the Nickel Plate Road at Fostoria, Ohio. But the largest share of coal traveled northwest to C&O's strategically located Presque Isle docks on Lake Erie's Maumee Bay near Toledo. This operation dwarfed even C&O's Newport News facilities for volume. In 1942, a car was emptied into waiting lake boats every 45 seconds, with an average of 2,150 cars handled daily. Farrington states that this accounted for 265,231 cars carrying 15,654,717 tons of coal in 1942 alone. C&O's 160-car trains weighing 13,500 tons left Russell behind one of the railroad's extremely powerful 2-10-4 Texas-type locomotives. After the war, C&O aggressively looked for new sources of coal traffic and volume, but Presque Isle peaked in 1950 at 17 million tons. Over the next few years traffic tapered off as a result of changing market conditions and in 1953 had leveled to 14 millions tons (though at peak times the dumpers still accommodated more than 2,000 tons daily). By this time, C&O was moving roughly 70 million tons of bituminous annually, 56 million from on-line mines.

After the war the markets for C&O coal evolved. The volume of coal used for domestic home heating declined, while coal for export increased dramatically. Farrington reports in his 1958 book *Railroads of the Hour* that during the mid-1950s, 14 percent of C&O's coal was destined for home heating, 14 percent was exported, and 18 percent was consumed by electric utilities. By the end of the decade, export coal was driving the market for Appalachian bituminous.

The C&O was famous for its massive Lima-built 2-6-6-6 Alleghenies that were among the largest and heaviest steam locomotives in the world, exceeding even Union Pacific's Big Boy in weight (a fact not recognized until years after their retirement). As one of America's leading bituminous haulers, C&O

refrained from dieselization longer than many other lines. During its peak, the railroad's steam locomotives consumed an estimated 2.6 million tons of coal annually. It was only in 1950 that C&O conceded to the efficiency of diesel-electric locomotives and began ordering new road diesels. Within a few years, the rule of the Allegheny types, Texas types, and other steam-era monsters had ended. The curious will find two 2-6-6-6s preserved: one at the Baltimore & Ohio Railroad Museum in Baltimore, the other at The Henry Ford museum in Dearborn, Michigan.

The old C&O has remained an important coal corridor to the present day, handling traffic for its successor, CSX.

Norfolk & Western

Norfolk & Western is enshrined in railroad mystique, not just for the coal it carried, but because it was the last railroad to surrender to diesel-electric motive power. Only in 1954 did N&W make the decision to convert to diesel operations, with its last steam running in 1960. While its famous passenger trains and home-built streamlined J-class 4-8-4s made it popular with the public and photographers, the railroad was also known for its massive late-era 2-8-8-2 Mallet-type locomotives, epitomized by the powerful Y6b and high-stepping A-class simple articulateds. These freight locomotives were beasts of burden used in the movement of N&W's lifeblood: coal.

Norfolk & Western predecessors traced their origins to 1838, but the railroad took its name in 1881, at a time when its forward-thinking vice president, Frederick J. Kimball, undertook the development of bituminous coalfields in southern Virginia, West Virginia, and eastern Kentucky. Over the next two decades, the railroad expanded rapidly, connecting the Virginia tidewater with those coalfields. N&W

Norfolk & Western Class Y No. 2142 leads a coal train at Blue Ridge Summit on July 31, 1958. The basis for N&W's highly successful Mallet was the United States Railroad Administration's World War I–era 2-8-8-2 design. N&W's Y6 class locomotives were often operated at just 20 to 30 miles per hour in heavy service but were capable of 50 miles per hour in mainline service. *Richard Jay Solomon*

began shipping coal in March 1883 and by 1887 was moving 1 million tons a year.

Key to N&W's success was reaching in a variety of directions to provide multiple conduits for its traffic. In 1890, through various line acquisitions, it reached northeasterly to Hagerstown, Maryland, and west to Columbus, Ohio; in the mid-1890s it expanded southward from Roanoke to North Carolina; and in 1901 it established a line to the Ohio River gateway

of Cincinnati. Meanwhile numerous branches were extended into the coalfields to tap mines.

N&W's coal operations were focused at its strategically placed marshaling and classification yards, where outbound carloads were gathered, sorted, and organized into enormous trains for mainline movement to markets at a multitude of destinations. Significant mainline mountain grades challenged its operations, and movement of heavy coal trains required extraordinary effort that resulted in the spectacular displays of steam power that made the railroad famous.

Opposite: This loaded N&W coal train stopped at Boaz, Virginia, east of Roanoke, to pick up a pusher for the climb up the Blue Ridge grade and is just rolling again with Class Y No. 2179 ahead of a Class A 2-6-6-4. *Jim Shaughnessy*

A brakeman prepares to jump off a slowing N&W coal train that has arrived at Boaz, Virginia, to cut on its pusher for the ascent of the Blue Ridge. A pair of N&W's massive Class Y Mallets waits to work the back of the coal train. *Jim Shaughnessy*

Norfolk & Western gathered coal from myriad mines in eight distinct districts. The largest concentration of coal was reached by branches radiating from its Pocahontas Division main line between Bluefield, West Virginia, and Williamson, Kentucky. At both of these locations, N&W's massive yards handled incoming loaded trains and outgoing empties, and the typical coal cycle began at one of these strategic staging points. S. Kip Farrington Jr. reports in *Railroading from the Rear End* that N&W's Bluefield dispatcher handled an average of 125 trains daily in 1946, many of them coal trains and locals for mines. A local from Bluefield would work up to a mine, drop empties, and collect loaded cars as well as paperwork for the number of cars needed by the mine the following day. Many mines would only fill a couple dozen cars, so it was normal for a local freight to make several stops during its run.

Coal moving east was delivered to Bluefield for weighing. From here, cars continued to Roanoke for classification and assembly into long trains for points north (toward Hagerstown) and south (toward North Carolina) on the Shenandoah Division, or east to the tidewater at Norfolk on the Norfolk Division. Eastbound trains from Roanoke crossed the Blue Ridge, where helpers were required to get trains over the grade.

Crewe, Virginia, 123.5 miles east of Roanoke—roughly the midway point to Norfolk—was where a crew change took place and also was the location of an important yard where trains were combined for the low-grade downhill run to the Atlantic seaboard. There, N&W's Lambert Point coal docks represented the most significant destination for coal departing the Roanoke yards. In 1945, Farrington wrote that 7 million tons a year were destined for transloading at Lambert Point. That seemed like an immense volume of coal for one location, yet it was only 19 percent of the estimated 54.4 million tons moved by N&W that year. At that time (and for most of the first half of the twentieth century), the greater share—68

Above: In the mid-1950s, the rise of export coal kept N&W busy moving heavy trains from West Virginia over the Blue Ridge to its Atlantic tidewater port at Lamberts Point, Virginia. Here, a pair of articulated locomotives makes for a spectacular show. In the lead is one of the railroad's famous Class Y Mallets. *Jim Shaughnessy*

Left: A Class Y Mallet works as a pusher on a Norfolk & Western coal train near Blue Ridge Summit east of Roanoke, Virginia. In the late 1950s, a booming export market resulted in a rising tide of coal moving east from the bituminous fields of West Virginia to tidewater ports. *Jim Shaughnessy*

percent—of N&W coal flowed westward from Appalachian mines.

That westbound coal was marshaled from Williamson and worked the N&W main line to Portsmouth, Ohio, where N&W operated an enormous classification yard built for the sole purpose of sorting coal cars from Appalachian mines. *Railway Age* reported in its September 12, 1955, issue that N&W's classification yard (and hump yard) constructed in 1928 was significantly expanded in 1955 to include a 13-track receiving yard and a new 35-track class yard. West of Portsmouth, coal was destined for the Great Lakes or Ohio River for transloading. Once past the mountains, N&W followed a river grade profile that allowed it to operate enormous trains. In the 1940s, these trains could be filled out to 13,000 tons; by the mid-1950s, trains were operated with up to about 200 cars and as much as 18,000 tons. This was enormously heavy at the time, since many railroads rarely operated freight trains of more than 4,000–5,000 tons.

The most difficult portion of N&W's main line was the eastward climb up the 2 percent Elkhorn Grade to the yard at Bluefield, elevation 2,556 feet above sea level. Bluefield sat in a saddle near the top of the Flat Top Mountain and developed as a railroad operations center in the late 1880s. As N&W's coal business grew, hauling trains over this grade became an increasingly difficult burden that forced the railroad to seek more efficient motive power. William D. Middleton distills N&W's efforts in his book *When the Steam Railroads Electrified*, explaining that prior to 1910 the railroad needed as many as six 2-8-0 Consolidations to lift 2,000-ton coal trains. With the advent of the Mallet articulated types, N&W bought 2-6-6-2s and later 2-8-8-2s to replace the Consolidations, but continued growth of the coal business, combined with other freight and passenger traffic, strained its largely double-track line to the limits of its capacity. The most serious impediment was the single-track, 3,014-foot Elkhorn Tunnel.

Fuel and water stops for locomotives added to N&W's capacity problems. In 1912, N&W decided

Above and top: Norfolk & Western was the last great steam show in the United States. On May 30, 1958, a Class Y 2-8-8-2 blackens the sky with coal dust and locomotive exhaust gases as it lifts a coal train toward Blue Ridge Summit. At the back, another Mallet works hard as a pusher to keep the coal moving. Ahead of the caboose are new and heavily laden 23300-series N&W hoppers. *Both photos Jim Shaughnessy*

to electrify its Elkhorn Grade using a high-voltage, single-phase, alternating-current transmission system derived from the New York, New Haven & Hartford's proven electrification. Twenty-seven miles of line from Vivian to Bluefield, West Virginia, were wired and composed 90 track miles including the double-track segments, passing sidings, and yard tracks. N&W's electrification was unusual in its application of a split-phase traction system supplied from a single-phase overhead.

N&W's first electric locomotives operated in 1914. According to Middleton, a pair of electrics was capable of lifting a 3,250-ton train up the Elkhorn Grade at a steady 14 miles per hour, nearly twice as fast as multiple Mallets working a 2,000-ton train. The electrification temporarily solved N&W's capacity problems and for the next 35 years worked the grade largely unremarked by the trade press. In the late 1940s, as part of a 5-mile line relocation that reduced the ruling grade to 1.4 percent, N&W bored

Norfolk & Western installed state-of-the-art electrification on 27 miles of line in 1912. Its boxcab electrics used phase splitters to convert single-phase AC to three-phase AC for synchronous induction traction motors. Power was transmitted from motors to drive wheels with jackshafts and side-rods. Eighty years later, Burlington Northern experimented with diesel-electrics using a modern three-phase AC system, and today AC-traction diesels are standard power on most coal lines (ironically, the major exception being N&W's successor, Norfolk Southern). *Jay Williams collection*

a new Elkhorn Tunnel more than twice as long as the original—7,052 feet. The new line allowed N&W to discontinue electrification, so in 1950 it made the unusual decision to replace electrics with steam power. Ten years later, the N&W acquired the largely parallel Virginian Railway for its superior eastward grade. By blending these two main lines, N&W was able to make the best advantage of ascending and descending grades in a manner that made for more efficient movement of coal.

The Virginian

The story of the Virginian Railway is atypical in American railroading. Financed by Henry Huttleson Rogers, a principal in Standard Oil, for the movement of Appalachian bituminous coal, the railroad began as a short line called the Deepwater Railway. In 1907, this was joined with the Tidewater Railway, another Rogers-backed venture, and the two became the Virginian Railway. The Virginian ran 443 miles from the mountain town of Deepwater by way of Roanoke to the tidewater port at Sewell's Point on Hampton Roads. Unlike many railroads, which rapidly expanded beyond their original plan or were melded into larger systems soon after tracks were laid, the Virginian achieved its essential form relatively quickly and remained that way for nearly half a century.

Largely parallel to Norfolk & Western, the Virginian tapped mines in the Pocahontas and New River districts. Except for a cluster of coal-hauling branches in the mountains near its western end, it had no other significant lines or feeders. One of its few extensions was a connection built in 1931 to facilitate interchange with New York Central.

The Virginian was superbly engineered and built to the heaviest standards of the time: 75,000-pound

On July 30, 1958, Virginian Railway EL-2B motor-generator electric No. 127 leads a long freight into the yards at Roanoke, Virginia. The Virginian operated 135 miles of electrified main line between Mullens, West Virginia, and Roanoke, Virginia, energized at 11,000 volts AC at 25Hz. Parallel Norfolk & Western merged with the Virginian in 1959, and electric operations were discontinued in 1962. *Richard Jay Solomon*

axle loads. Its main line was characterized by gentle curves; tall, steel tower–supported plate-girder trestles; and numerous tunnels—34 on its main line and 14 on coal feeders.

Early on, the railroad was famous for its enormously heavy trains. Although its single-track main was equipped with sidings that limited train length to 170 cars, its high-axle load, pioneering use of gigantic six-axle hoppers carrying up to 120 tons of coal, and other high-capacity cars allowed the Virginian to run trains up to 9,000 tons before World War I.

Moving such heavy trains in the steam era required exceptional locomotives. Virginian's most difficult operation was its eastward climb from Elmore to Clarks Gap, West Virginia, where the ruling grade exceeded 2 percent. In *When the Steam Railroads Electrified*,

William D. Middleton explains that to move a 5,500-ton coal train, Virginian assigned some of the largest steam locomotives of the time: massive 2-8-8-2 Mallet compounds to lead and a pair of even larger 2-10-10-2 Mallets as rear-end helpers. Virginian even bought a Triplex-type locomotive (three sets of driving wheels) in an effort to gain more power from a single boiler.

In the 1920s, with its coal traffic rising and the railroad looking to achieve even greater efficiency, the Virginian emulated N&W's lead by installing high-voltage, alternating-current electrification on its western grades. Wires were energized at 11,000 volts at 25 cycles. The first electrics went into service in 1925, and by 1926 wires extended over 134 miles of line between Mullens, West Virginia, and Roanoke, Virginia. This was substantially more extensive than N&W's similar electrification, and power was supplied by a railroad-operated generating station at Narrows, Virginia. The Virginian's original electric engines were near duplicates of N&W's and used a split-phase jackshaft propulsion system.

In 1924, on the eve of its electrification, the Virginian hauled 7.4 million tons of coal. Four years later, it carried 11.8 million tons, and by 1948 it was moving 15.5 million tons annually. Increased volume led it to buy enormous motor-generator electrics custom-built by General Electric in 1948. These stream-lined units used eight axles in a B-B+B-B arrangement and were typically operated in semi-permanently coupled pairs. Each mated pair weighed 1,033,832 pounds, delivered 260,000 pounds of starting tractive effort, and produced 6,800 horsepower, with a maximum speed of 50 miles per hour. In 1955, the Virginian ordered a dozen Ignitron rectifiers from GE to finally replace its three-phase, side-rod electrics in heavy coal service. Designated EL-C, the GE rectifiers were delivered over the next two years and were much like contemporary high-output diesels.

GIGANTIC SIX-AXLE HOPPERS HELPED THE VIRGINIAN TO RUN COAL TRAINS UP TO 9,000 TONS BEFORE WORLD WAR I.

On its non-electrified lines, the Virginian continued to push the limits of steam. In the mid-1940s, it ordered near copies of Chesapeake & Ohio's massive 2-6-6-6 Alleghenies, making it the only other railroad to use this type. In the 1950s, it dieselized with Fairbanks-Morse opposed-piston-type locomotives, including F-M's extraordinarily powerful Train Masters that delivered 2,400 horsepower per unit (substantially more than the Electro-Motive GP9s ordered by N&W and rated at just 1,750 horsepower).

The Virginian's Sewalls Point (sometimes "Sewell's") coal piers served a purpose equivalent to N&W's Lambert Point and C&O's Newport News facilities. An article in the *1955 Keystone Coal Buyers Manual* details the Virginian's facility, which consisted of two coal piers. Pier 1 had low-level loading equipment to minimize degradation of coal from the effects of dropping. This could load up to 2,500 tons per hour. Pier 2 was adjacent to it and substantially larger. At 1,074 feet long and with a pair of double-car dumpers, it was capable of loading up to three vessels simultaneously and transloaded up to 7,200 tons of coal an hour. In addition to loading Virginian coal, Sewalls Point also moved traffic interchanged via the New York Central.

The Virginian's route that was parallel to N&W featured superior grades and lucrative coal traffic that made it an ideal candidate for inclusion in N&W's system. Merger was first considered in the mid-1920s and finally accomplished more than 30 years later, at the end of 1959. Although portions of its main line were abandoned, most made excellent additions to N&W's coal operation and allowed N&W to establish uni-direction main lines to make best use of grades and track capacity. In the process, N&W discontinued the Virginian's electrification in 1962. The Sewalls Point facility was also closed.

At the back of a northbound PRR coal train, a Class I1 2-10-0 works as a helper shoving against an N5 cabin (commonly known as a caboose). Another Decapod works the head end. In the 1950s, rivers of bituminous coal flowed north over the Elmira Branch to Sodus Point and other connections in New York state. *Jim Shaughnessy*

The Pennsylvania Railroad

In its heyday, the Pennsylvania Railroad was the largest and most intensive railroad in North America and one of the largest conveyors of bituminous coal. Anthracite coal became an important source of traffic for PRR and its affiliated lines before the Civil War. After the war, between the 1880s and early years of the twentieth century, PRR built, bought, and extended numerous lines to tap new sources of coal

across the rich bituminous fields in central and western Pennsylvania. Much of this coal was consumed by the burgeoning steel industry that developed in the valleys around Pittsburgh and Johnstown, and in the West Virginia panhandle and eastern Ohio.

Bituminous coal also flowed along various corridors to reach markets beyond PRR lines. PRR's Northern Central developed first as an anthracite corridor but later provided important paths for bituminous coal. One of the best-known Northern Central coal operations was the Elmira Branch, which forwarded coal from central Pennsylvania mines north to the Lake Ontario port at Sodus Point and made connections with New York Central. Sodus Point was developed as a coal port in 1884

In November 1947, Pennsylvania Railroad I1s Decapod No. 4344 leads a westbound freight at BF near Sugar Run, working toward the summit at Gallitzin, Pennsylvania. In consist is a mix of empty coal hoppers and other freight. *Bruce Fales, Jay Williams collection*

and in its early years handled up to 150,000 tons of bituminous and anthracite coal annually, much of which then moved via lake boats to Canadian markets. The growth of this coal route continued well into the twentieth century, encouraging PRR to expand capacity on the Elmira Branch and Sodus Point docks. Authors Charles S. Roberts and David W. Messer report in their book, *Triumph VII: Harrisburg to the Lakes, Wilkes-Barre, Oil City and Red Bank*, that by 1911 Sodus Point was handling 5 million tons of coal annually. In the late 1920s, PRR rebuilt and expanded the pier. It measured 885 feet long and 58 feet high and contained eight coal pockets that allowed two lake boats to take coal simultaneously. In conjunction with pier expansion, yard capacity at Sodus was expanded to hold up to 800 cars. Facilities were further expanded during World War II and again in 1952. Yards feeding the Elmira Branch were essential to efficient operation

of coal traffic. Southport Yard near Elmira, New York, had capacity for 1,625 cars.

Traffic moving via the Elmira Branch came from several directions. Many coal trains reached the branch via Tyrone, moving northeastward on the Bald Eagle Branch to Lock Haven, then on to Williamsport, Pennsylvania. Other trains moved east on the old Philadelphia & Erie via Keating, Renovo, and Lock Haven, or traveled northward on the Northern Central via Sunbury and North-umberland, Pennsylvania.

Although Sodus was the most significant destination, coal was also interchanged with New York Central at Canandaigua, New York, and in later

On July 4, 1956, a PRR Decapod shoves coal hoppers to the dumpers on the Sodus Point Pier. Coal is loaded into a waiting lake boat below. *Jim Shaughnessy*

years at Himrod Junction with NYC's Fallbrook Route and at Newark, New York, with its West Shore Route. Elmira was another important interchange point. Bill Caloroso notes in his book *Pennsylvania Railroad's Elmira Branch* that PRR classified nearly all coal moving over the line at the strategically situated Southport Yards and made connections there with the Erie Railroad, the Delaware Lackawanna & Western, and the Lehigh Valley.

In 1940, PRR began shipping coal via Sodus Point to the Niagara Hudson power plant at Oswego. Traffic boomed on the Elmira Branch in the 1950s, with as many as six loaded trains moving over the line every 24 hours. It was one of the last places where

PRR worked steam, assigning its hefty I1s Decapods ("s" for "superheated") fore and aft on both coal and merchandise trains. Steam ended in 1957, and within just a decade this whole corridor dried up, largely due to the opening of the St. Lawrence Seaway in 1959. As late as 1965, PRR was transloading more than a million tons a year at Sodus Point. However, by 1967, the dock's last active season, only 123,454 tons were handled there, according to the *1970 Coal Traffic Annual*.

Opposite: Iron ore is unloaded from lake steamship *Edward Townsend* at Erie, Pennsylvania. Pennsylvania Railroad's Philadelphia & Erie affiliate developed expanded coal piers at this port during the second half of the nineteenth century. This remained an active transloading point until the 1960s, when it closed in favor of New York Central's Lake Erie piers at Ashtabula, Ohio. *PRR photo, P. C. Auction, Railroad Museum of Pennsylvania, PHMC*

Pennsylvania Railroad's Western New York & Pennsylvania route over Keating Summit between Olean, New York, and Emporium, Pennsylvania, was one of several significant mainline helper operations on the system. This view shows a coal train at Keating Summit. *Railroad Museum of Pennsylvania, PHMC*

In addition to Elmira Branch traffic, PRR coal moved east from large yards at Northumberland and Williamsport to various gateways. Trains went via Sunbury on the Susquehanna River over the old North and West Branch Railway to Wilkes-Barre, Pennsylvania, where PRR interchanged with the Delaware & Hudson and other carriers. Also important was the branch to Shamokin—parallel to a Reading Company route—that enabled PRR to move coal eastward via a connection with the Lehigh Valley.

PRR moved coal to other Great Lakes destinations via its Philadelphia & Erie and Western New York & Pennsylvania routes. The P&E had reached its western terminus and namesake by 1860 and constructed significant lake piers in 1867. In the

early years, anthracite accounted for 75 percent of the coal traffic moving via Erie, Pennsylvania. Under PRR's stewardship, P&E expanded the coal piers during the second half of the nineteenth century. Roberts and Messer note that these facilities were upgraded and expanded several times to accommodate increased volumes of traffic. In 1887, the docks were improved to handle incoming iron ore as well as outgoing coal. By 1910, the docks at Erie could accommodate up to 440 cars and 28,000 tons daily. PRR also moved coal to Buffalo, largely to serve steel mills and related industries. In Ohio, PRR's Sandusky Branch grew as a coal route after 1902, running from Columbus to coal docks at its namesake on Lake Erie. In 1964, PRR sold this line to the Norfolk & Western in a deal that was a prelude to the Penn Central merger and key to N&W's acquisition of the Nickel Plate Road and the Wabash Railroad.

At one time, PRR routes moved considerable tonnage through eastern seaboard ports, notably Baltimore, New York, and Philadelphia. In 1965 (as reported by *1970 Coal Traffic Annual*) PRR moved nearly 6.9 million tons through these ports, with the largest share transloaded through the port of New York. Traffic declined dramatically in the Penn Central era. By that time, the railroad had ceased to transload coal at New York, and the *1975 Coal Traffic Annual* reported that only 415,523 tons moved through Philadelphia and just over 1 million tons through Baltimore, despite Penn Central originating nearly 37.4 million tons of bituminous coal in 1974.

Top and bottom left: Under a cloud of its own exhaust, PRR Decapod No. 4311 labors upgrade on the Elmira Branch near Roaring Branch, Pennsylvania, on May 5, 1957. This coal train is destined for Sodus Point, New York. The head end is only part of the show—at the back are another Decapod and a pair of demoted Alco PA diesels. Few railroads used PAs in freight service, but PRR, dissatisfied with the locomotives' reliability in passenger service, re-geared them for freight work and assigned them to helper service on the Elmira Branch for a few years. *Both photos Jim Shaughnessy*

Chapter 3 MODERN APPALACHIAN BITUMINOUS COAL

Chesapeake & Ohio B30-7 5531 leads a loaded coal train at "KV" cabin on the Kanawha subdivision at Kenova, West Virginia, in November 1987. *Mike Abalos*

Since the end of the steam era, there have been significant changes in the mining, movement, and consumption of bituminous coal from the Appalachian region, including numerous railroad mergers, line consolidation, and route abandonment. Some lines that were once busy coal corridors are now little more than bike paths, while other routes have blossomed or been rebuilt as coal conduits.

Most of the traditional coal-hauling railroads have been combined into larger companies. Chesapeake & Ohio, Baltimore & Ohio, and Western Maryland, which became the Chessie System in 1972, were further melded with the Family Lines/Seaboard System railroads in the 1980s to form the giant CSX network. Likewise, in the 1960s, Norfolk & Western absorbed the Virginian, Nickel Plate Road, and Wabash Railroad, and then in 1982 merged with Southern Railway to form Norfolk Southern. Pennsylvania Railroad and New York Central merged in 1968 to form Penn Central; New Haven joined the fray in 1969, and by 1970 the entire railroad descended into a financial quagmire unrivaled until the Enron debacle. Penn Central and other bankrupt carriers, including most of the surviving anthracite lines, were reorganized by an act of Congress and combined to form Conrail in 1976. Key to Conrail's early strategy was greater volumes of coal traffic, but by the late 1970s this had failed to develop, and massive government investment was required to keep the railroad alive. The Staggers Act of 1980, which deregulated much of the American railroad network, combined with clever management by L. Stanley Crane, made Conrail profitable by the mid-1980s. From the mid-1980s, Conrail was subject to repeated acquisition efforts, and finally in 1998 and 1999, the property was acquired and divided by CSX and NS. By that time its route structure had been much altered.

Economies of scale favoring large mines and large consumers have been the trend in Appalachian coal railroading since the end of the steam era. The development of the unit train in the late 1950s and early 1960s was first applied to eastern bituminous mines and has

The Chessie System used former Chesapeake & Ohio Lima-built 4-8-4 No. 614 in a series of high-profile coal-service tests in January 1985, nearly 30 years after C&O had concluded regular steam freight operations. A westbound empty train charges passed Handley, West Virginia, on January 10, 1985. *George W. Kowanski*

become the predominant method of transporting coal by rail throughout the United States. As a result, many yards once used to gather and classify coal cars have been downsized, abandoned, or converted for other uses. Today, coal trains typically operate directly from large mines to end destinations, whether electrical-generation stations or large marine terminals.

Air-quality legislation, growing demand for electricity, and the complex dynamics of the international energy and steelmaking markets have all affected where coal is mined and delivered. Some traditional coal-mining areas had effectively closed down by the mid-1990s, leaving once-busy coal lines

largely devoid of this traditional traffic. In some situations, lines that relied entirely on coal were abandoned and tracks removed. Yet, further market changes in more recent years have seen a revival of coal traffic. Routes previously given up for dead have come back to life. At the same time, demand for low-sulfur western coal has penetrated eastern markets; where coal from Appalachia was once shipped across the country, now it is not unusual to find unit trains of western coal serving power plants across the East.

Technological changes, including aluminum coal cars, radio-controlled remote diesels, advances in microprocessor-controlled alternating-current traction systems, and, most recently, the advent of commercial electronically controlled pneumatic (ECP) brakes have changed the way railroads move coal, as well as the appearance of coal trains. The days of rusty cuts of banged-up steel hoppers have given way to long, clean unit trains of high-volume aluminum cars.

Above: Detroit Edison empty unit train UDM-97C rolls east on Conrail's Water Level Route at Berea, Ohio, en route to the mines in southwestern Pennsylvania on August 24, 1991. In the lead are DE U30Cs Nos. 020 and 008 and Conrail Nos. 6593 and 6495, followed by 62 125-ton hoppers, 3 more DE locomotives (Nos. 015, 010, and 009), and 73 more 125-ton cars. Detroit Edison was one of the early utilities to purchase both its own cars and locomotives. The trains operated with mid-train radio-controlled slave locomotives. *Doug Eisele*

Left: A southbound Seaboard System unit coal train rolls south on the former Louisville & Nashville main line between Cincinnati and Atlanta at Morley, Tennessee, in May 1986. The train is exiting Hickory Creek Tunnel, and in a few miles it will stop at Chaska, Tennessee, to take on a pusher for the stiff climb over Duff Mountain. *Scott R. Snell*

The Clinchfield

The Clinchfield had its genesis in a late-nineteenth-century plan by ex–Union general John Wilder to tap coalfields in Virginia and eastern Kentucky. Although his plans were undone by the panic of 1893, Boston financier Charles Hellier stepped in to reorganize the Wilder's Charleston, Cincinnati & Chicago Railroad as the Ohio River & Charleston Railroad Company. In his book *The Clinchfield Railroad in the Coal Fields*, Robert A. Helm notes that Hellier had substantial holdings in coal reserves along the Ohio River.

On a cool morning in Erwin, Tennessee, Clinchfield U36C No. 3602 and a pair of SD40s lead a coal train bound for the Duke Power Plant. Clinchfield purchased seven GE U36Cs in 1971—the only GE power on this otherwise all-Electro-Motive railroad. Their stint on the line was relatively short—by 1977 they had been traded to affiliate Seaboard Coast Line in exchange for SD45s. *Unknown photographer, Tom Kline collection*

George L. Carter picked up the pieces of earlier lines in 1902 and in 1908 consolidated them as the Carolina, Clinchfield & Ohio, which became more commonly known as the Clinchfield. The railroad's predecessors had laid out steep, tortuous, and poorly engineered lines. Under Carter's administration, the railroad was rebuilt and realigned to reduce gradient and curvature. The resulting north–south line was built to modern and exceptionally high standards that required significant investment. As originally conceived, the modern line used numerous tall, tower-supported, plate-girder steel trestles and frequent tunnels to keep grades to a minimum. To reach a connection with the Chesapeake & Ohio, the Clinchfield was extended 35 miles northward from Dante, Virginia, to a junction at Elkhorn City,

Kentucky. The line was opened in February 1915 and featured the most difficult construction on the railroad.

Elkhorn City developed as the line's most important interchange. Other important interchange points were located at St. Paul, Virginia (with the Norfolk & Western); Miller Yard, Virginia (with the Louisville & Nashville and a regional line called the Interstate); Johnson City, Tennessee (with the Southern Railway); Bostic, North Carolina (with the Seaboard Air Line); and its southern terminal, Spartanburg, South Carolina (with the Southern Railway and the Atlantic Coast Line).

Lucrative coal traffic and the strategic north–south nature of the Clinchfield made it a profitable and desirable property. In 1924, the Atlantic Coast Line and the Louisville & Nashville signed a joint 999-year lease on the Clinchfield, with Clinchfield operating 317 miles, the majority of the main line. The Clinchfield maintained an independent appearance into the 1970s, and like other ACL and L&N properties was a component of the Family Lines, then the Seaboard System, before becoming part of CSX at the end of 1982.

As sanders dust mainline rails, two Clinchfield GP7s and F7s roar out of Kingsport, Tennessee, with an early unit coal train in March 1967. To the left, on the adjacent track, strings of empty coal hoppers await their return to nearby coal mines. The peaked extensions on the hoppers' ends increase the volume of coal they can carry. Today, the Italianate-style passenger depot seen on the right survives as a bank, while the old Clinchfield is operated by CSX and hosts heavy traffic volumes. *Unknown photographer, Tom Kline collection*

A pair of Lehigh Valley "Snow Birds" (Alco C-628s) leads a 157-car coal train at Allentown, Pennsylvania, on May 11,1972. In 1976, Lehigh Valley was among the railroads absorbed into Conrail. *Doug Eisele*

Baltimore & Ohio SD50 No. 8593 leads empty coal cars west over the Potomac River at Harpers Ferry, West Virginia, on March 21, 1986. East of Cumberland, Maryland, it was standard practice for a single six-motor unit to move as many as 200 empty cars, although this train has just 163 empties. *Doug Eisele*

Moving Coal on the Old West End

Although the original Baltimore & Ohio route is not as busy as it was in its heyday, CSX still originates significant volumes of coal on former B&O lines. Much of this coal is shipped eastward to Mid-Atlantic utility customers and for export via East Coast ports.

A good example of early-twenty-first-century operations on CSX's Mountain Subdivision was unit coal train T861, known colloquially as the Whitetail because it loaded at the Alpha Natural Resources Whitetail Mine near Newburg, West Virginia. This typical "steam coal" unit train consisted of 80 loaded hoppers and weighed 10,500 tons. Where trains on the old C&O often weigh more than twice as much as this because of that route's superior profile, coal

trains on the old B&O are limited by severe grades and curvature. This route remains challenging despite the advent of modern locomotives, and helpers are still needed uphill. The descent of the legendary Seventeen Mile Grade from Altamont, Maryland, to Keyser, West Virginia, is no less treacherous with heavier modern trains. Today, the descent is limited to 10 miles per hour as a result of a fatal runaway in 2000 (B&O's runaway tracks had been removed many years earlier).

There have been changes over the years. Keyser Yard is just a remnant of its former greatness, since B&O coal now moves in unit trains and no longer requires classification. East of Keyser, the train continues to Cumberland, since the old Paterson Creek Cutoff was abandoned decades ago in part of a move to downsize B&O's physical plant. East of Cumberland, T861 follows the former B&O main line east through Harpers Ferry and Brunswick to the Constellation Energy plant at Dickerson, Maryland.

Working east at the Kingwood Tunnel in Tunnelton, West Virginia, on October 15, 1994, the head end of a CSX unit train led by C30-7 No. 7042 has just topped the Newberg Grade and is beginning its descent of the Cheat River Grade. Shoving hard at the back is a three-unit helper. Short, heavy trains combined with the sawtooth profile of the Mountain Sub have made for very challenging operations over the years. *Brian Solomon*

Sun burns off the morning fog on October 18, 2002, as "coal cars" (as empty coal trains are known on the B&O) roll west through the old yards at Keyser, West Virginia. Once an important marshaling point, today Keyser is essentially a holding area for unit coal trains coming east from Grafton, West Virginia. *Brian Solomon*

The Fall and Rise of Export Coal

The bituminous export boom that had supported the Appalachian railroads for much of second half of the twentieth century began to ebb in the late 1990s, causing concern among industry leaders. Changes outside the United States had more to do with this sag in traffic than any inherent problems with the railroads. In the May 2, 1999, edition of the *Washington Post*, veteran transportation reporter Don Phillips says, "The decline in export coal began with the Asian financial crisis. It was also complicated by myriad economic and political factors, including overcapacity in Australian mines, the unusually strong dollar, the end of apartheid in South Africa, economic chaos in ocean shipping, steel dumping by Eastern Europe, and even the revival of 'mom-and-pop' coke production in China." According to the National Mining Association, export coal shipments peaked in 1996 at around 79 million tons but then slid to just 60 million tons in 1998.

Most of the decline was in coal used for electricity production, but metallurgical coal used to make coke for use in basic steelmaking declined as well. David

Left: In March 2004, CSX AC4400CW No. 525, leading northbound empties, meets southbound loads at Woodbine on CSX's KD Sub south of Corbin, Kentucky (the initials KD are derived from the old Knoxville Division). The train loaded CSX's EK (Eastern Kentucky) Subdivision, which connects with the KD Sub at Patio (an important junction in Winchester). *Marshall W. Beecher*

Below: In 2008, Western New York & Pennsylvania Railroad handled coal shipments to the S. A. Carlson Electric generating station that formerly moved by truck. The plant's four boilers can consume up to 400 tons of coal per day at peak times and supply electricity and steam to a district heating system in the city of Jamestown, New York. In late 2008, WNY&P moved approximately 12 cars a week from Allegheny Resources (which loads at the former PRR yard at Emporium) to Jamestown via Olean. *Patrick Yough*

Portions of the former C&O main line have been converted from directional double-track to single-track under Centralized Traffic Control. A westbound empty train has stopped at "OX" cabin near Moss Run, Virginia, on the afternoon of November 26, 2005, to meet an eastbound loaded unit train CSX U729-24 led by SD70MAC No. 4733. CSX's U729 handles coal from Raders Run near Rupert, West Virginia, bound for tidewater shipment at Newport News. *T. S. Hoover*

Above: A pair of CSX AC4400CWs leads train symbol T720-20 on CSX's former Chesapeake & Ohio main line at Fort Spring, West Virginia, on December 2, 2004. The train loaded at Magnum Coal's Toms Fork, West Virginia, mine and is destined for the Dominion Terminal (formerly operated by C&O) at Newport News, Virginia *T. S. Hoover*

Next page: Norfolk Southern B32-8 No. 3563 leads a loaded train through a curve with an old mainline coaling station. N&W's Mallets may be history, but vestiges of the steam era survive on the old N&W main line, and the coal continues to flow. *Scott R. Snell*

Goode, then Norfolk Southern chairman, told the *Washington Post*, "In my 30-year career, I've seen people give up on coal maybe eight or 10 times, and it's always been wrong, and I think they're wrong again."

The export coal cycle had an effect on domestic railroading that went well beyond the movement of coal. It was during this time that NS was again considering an attempt to purchase Conrail. In his book *The Men Who Loved Trains*, Rush Loving Jr. points out:

> Norfolk Southern was beginning to need Conrail for a reason so secret that only a few people inside NS and the coal industry knew it. The railroad's legendary profit center, the export

coal business from Appalachia, was not as healthy as it appeared. The coalfields in southern West Virginia and southwest Virginia were being depleted. Coal seams were narrow, making the mines less competitive. Furthermore, the market in Europe was being invaded by South Africans, who now had a new rail line linking their mines to their export piers. In Britain the mines were closing down, and people outside and inside Norfolk Southern were expecting the utilities there and on the continent to use Appalachian coal, but European visitors were telling McClellan they planned to convert their boilers and use gas from the North Sea....

Above: Coal is the predominant commodity moved by rail and barge along the Monongahela River south of Pittsburgh, Pennsylvania. At Greenfield Bend at Coal Center, Pennsylvania, northbound Norfolk Southern train N21-16 led by former Conrail SD80MACs—Nos. 7206, 7208, and 7205—brings 130 cars to the Keystone generating station in Shelocta, Pennsylvania. Campbell Transportation Company towboat *Richard C.* is heading upriver with nine empty hopper barges in tow for Foundation Coal's river load-out at Grays Landing, Pennsylvania. On the east side of the river is CSX's Mon Subdivision. *Eric M. Johnson*

Right: A pair of Louisville & Nashville Alco-built C-420s leads a Falcon Mine run south of Hazard, Kentucky, in May 1980. *George S. Pitarys.*

Above: Ohio Central operates a shuttle train for American Electric Power's Conesville generating station near Zanesville, Ohio. The train makes a short run to deliver coal to the plant from several online mines in the Cadiz, Ohio, area in southeastern Ohio near Wheeling, West Virginia. In this view, Ohio Central No. 4026 is on an empty shuttle returning to the mines for reloading. *Mark Leppert*

Left: In the 1960s the Pennsylvania Railroad wanted to build a new facility at Erie, Pennsylvania, but was denied permission by the city. Instead, a new facility was constructed at Ashtabula Harbor, Ohio. The facility became Conrail property in 1976, and in 1998–1999 Conrail was divided by Norfolk Southern and CSX. Presently, Ashtabula Harbor is used by both NS and CSX. This July 1998 photo depicts cuts of Conrail hoppers waiting for dumping and returning to the mines for reloading. *Marshall W. Beecher*

If NS lost its export market, it would have few U.S. customers to whom it could shift the coal. CSX had more coal reserves and served more power plants than NS. "We had a big deficit, if you count the coal service area that we had as opposed to CSX," said Goode. Conrail would provide Norfolk Southern with a wider base of customers and access to the more efficient mines of central West Virginia and Monongahela in southwestern Pennsylvania, thereby giving NS parity with CSX.

The details of the battle between CSX and NS for the control and ultimately the division of Conrail have been well documented, but it was the fears of a declining export coal market that urged the eastern giants to action.

In 1997, prior to its Conrail acquisitions, CSX handled roughly 250 coal trains daily. The export market proved cyclical, and despite declines in the 1990s, within a few years, global changes in the energy market resulted in a heightened demand for export coal. In 2000, CSX moved 1,660,000 carloads of coal, accounting for 25 percent of the railroad's revenue. In 2002, coal represented 41.5 percent of its originating tonnage. Today, CSX moves coal to waterfront piers at Baltimore, Newport News, and Mobile, Alabama, for transloading to ships.

Results of the Conrail Split

Despite declines in demand for Appalachian coal, Conrail remained a formidable coal hauler into the 1990s. As late as 1992, Conrail was originating more than 320,000 coal cars annually and serving numerous coal customers along its lines. While Conrail's other traffic made it an attractive acquisition to Norfolk Southern and CSX, the benefits of a split to large coal producers and coal customers were key during negotiations.

The acquisition, division, and subsequent integration of Conrail routes by CSX and Norfolk Southern during 1998–1999 resulted in a variety of changes to bituminous coal movement in the eastern United States. Coal customers served by CSX and Norfolk Southern benefited from single-line access to highly productive mines on the former Monongahela Railway served by Conrail. This was absorbed by NS, with CSX granted loading rights to all the affected mines. In a related move, CSX rebuilt its former Pittsburgh & Lake Erie yard at Newell, Pennsylvania, to serve as a staging yard for unit coal trains. Today, CSX crews bring empty hopper trains to Newell to hand over to NS crews for loading on the former Monongahela. NS then returns loaded CSX trains to Newell for CSX crews to forward for delivery to customers. In addition, CSX was granted running rights on the former Monongahela Railway East Division (between Newell and Catawba Junction, West Virginia, near Fairmont) to reach former B&O lines radiating from Grafton, West Virginia.

Power plants on former Conrail lines benefited from the split by gaining lower-cost, single-line access to highly desirable compliance (low-sulfur) coal mines served by CSX and NS in the central Appalachian region. Cheaper access to compliance coal allowed power plants to avoid costs associated with installing flue gas desulphurization systems (FGD, commonly known as scrubbers) necessary to comply with more stringent antipollution laws imposed on the burning of high-sulfur coal.

Pennsylvania Power & Light

Prior to the split of Conrail, Pennsylvania Power & Light (PP&L) was the railroad's largest coal customer. Significantly, PP&L had been one of the earliest unit train customers and first received unit trains in 1964 from Conrail predecessor, Pennsylvania Railroad. These originally operated between a Barnes & Tucker mine on PRR's Susquehanna Extension Branch, compass north of Cresson (where the branch joined the main line), and the Martins Creek Steam Electric Station along the Delaware River north of Easton, Pennsylvania. The success of this pioneering unit train service encouraged PP&L to expand unit train operations and acquire its own fleet of coal cars. Where railroads traditionally provided hoppers, PP&L was among the early utilities to invest in its own equipment, gradually assembling a fleet of more than 1,000 100-ton, three-bay, steel hoppers to serve all three coal-fired generating stations in Pennsylvania: Martins Creek, Brunner Island near York, and Montour (commonly known as

PP&L WAS AMONG THE FIRST UTILITIES TO INVEST IN ITS OWN COAL CARS, ASSEMBLING A FLEET OF MORE THAN 1,000 100-TON, THREE-BAY, STEEL HOPPERS.

Conrail SD40-2s lead westbound train WHCL12 on Track 3 at South Fork, Pennsylvania, on October 16, 1994. Originally, the train was to load for Strawberry Ridge at one of the mines in the Clearfield area but was reassigned to load at a mine on the former Monongahela Railway for the power plant at York Haven, Pennsylvania, south of Harrisburg. *Patrick Yough*

Strawberry Ridge). To ensure a constant supply of fuel, PP&L also invested in coal reserves and operated its own mines in western and central Pennsylvania. Its Marion mine at Tunnelton was one of the first coal mines built specifically to load unit trains in motion and was equipped with a loop track that connected with PRR's Conemaugh Line near Saltsburg.

PP&L-owned mines survived until the late 1980s when the market changed as a result of a Pennsylvania Public Utility Commission ruling that required PP&L and other utilities to buy coal from the lowest-cost producer. This changed traffic flowing to PP&L plants because the new Bailey Mine offered the lowest-cost coal. Bailey is one of the largest underground mines in the United States, producing as much as 10 million tons annually.

PP&L's switch to Bailey coal benefited Conrail by giving the railroad a longer haul, since Bailey was farther from the power plants than PP&L's mines in the Clearfield area, yet costing substantially less to move. To deliver and load trains at Clearfield-

area mines had required two train crews, while tight curvature and stiff grades required a power-intensive operation. By comparison, the run from Bailey Mine to the plants followed river valleys between Waynesburg and Johnstown. This gentler route could be served with a single train crew working from the Shire Oaks coal-staging yard and Conrail's Altoona hub.

Of interest, were PP&L Strawberry Ridge trains destined for the Montour plant. These operated east from Altoona on the old PRR main line to Tyrone and then joined the former PRR Bald Eagle Branch, now maintained by the Nittany & Bald Eagle between Tyrone and Lock Haven. (Although traditionally a coal route, part of this branch had been discontinued early in the Conrail era and was revived in the 1990s.) At Lock Haven, PP&L trains joined the former PRR Buffalo Line and continued east to a junction at Watsontown. From there they reached the plant by

Conrail SD60 No. 6863 leads a unit train loading at CONSOL Energy's Blacksville No. 2 Mine in Wana, West Virginia, on November 12, 1994. Blacksville No. 2 was one of the two mines on the former Monongahela Railway to load the original Detroit Edison unit train that served the generating station at Monroe, Michigan. *Mark Leppert*

another former PRR line, known by Conrail as the Washingtonville Secondary

When the Clean Air Act (pages 84-85) went into effect in 1995, PP&L initially chose not to install flue gas desulphurization systems at its plants and instead resorted to buying central Appalachian compliance coal located on both NS and CSX lines to blend with locally mined coal from the Clearfield area. Compliance coal is defined by creating pollution levels less than prescribed limits, specifically an emission rate of sulfur dioxide (SO_2) values of less than 1.2 pounds of SO_2 per million BTU. Compliance coal was interchanged with Conrail at

CSX AC4400CW No. 29 leads GALX empty hoppers on the former Louisville & Nashville Lotts Creek Branch past the wooden AJAX coal tipple at Bulan, near Hazard, Kentucky. The train is en route to Little Elk Mining's loader at Sigmon, Kentucky, in May 1998. *William M. Beecher*

Hagerstown, Maryland, for forwarding to PP&L plants. However, Conrail and PP&L disagreed on the rate structure, resulting in a PP&L suit with the Surface Transportation Board against Conrail.

The differences between the railroad and PP&L regarding shipping rates were resolved, and the utility gained single-line access to mines in West Virginia and was promised lower freight rates. In return for a promise of better service, PP&L emerged as an early endorser of the Conrail split, and NS emerged as the coal supplier to all three PP&L plants.

Further changes to PP&L moves occurred in the late 1990s as the Commonwealth of Pennsylvania

moved toward electricity deregulation, which resulted in changes to the PP&L corporate structure. Today the generating stations are managed by a company called PPL Generation.

In early 2007, PPL Generation took delivery of approximately 650 aluminum BethGonII rotary gondolas from FreightCar America. These were built at the former Norfolk Southern car shops in Roanoke, Virginia. In 2008, PPL Generation commissioned FGD systems at their Brunner Island and Montour stations. Since limestone is a key ingredient in the operation of modern FGD systems, PPL Generation freed up several trainsets of its older steel hoppers to haul unit limestone trains to the plants.

As recently as 2008, some unit trains destined for the PPL Generation plants and loading in West Virginia have used Norfolk Southern's former Conrail West Virginia secondary (once a New York

On November 26, 2006, Buffalo & Pittsburgh SD45 No. 460 leads an empty coal train across the massive former Buffalo, Rochester & Pittsburgh Allegheny River Bridge at Mosgrove, Pennsylvania. As described by its symbol—RINC (Riker Yard to New Castle–CSX Interchange)—the train is destined for interchange at CSX's New Castle, Pennsylvania, yard. It traveled via CSX and the former Monongahela Railway for loading at the Federal No. 2 Mine at Miracle Run, West Virginia. When loaded, the train will return to B&P for delivery to Midwest Generation's Homer City generating station. *Mark Leppert*

Central route) via Dickinson, West Virginia, to join Ohio Central's former PRR Panhandle Line at Columbus. They run east on the Panhandle to a point just west of Mingo Junction, Ohio, where they are routed onto NS's River Line and Bayard Branch to Conway, Pennsylvania, and then east over the former PRR Main Line to Altoona and beyond to their respective destinations.

Due to tight clearances on the rotary car dumper at Strawberry Ridge, Conrail and NS have used a variety of dedicated locomotives on the unit trains over the years. Initially, in the late 1970s, Conrail assigned a pool of 25 GP38-2s (Nos. 8040–8064)

and 8 SD40-2s (Nos. 6385–6389 and 6391–6393). Later, 12 more SD40-2s (Nos. 6399–6410) were added to the pool. All had their snowplows trimmed

Above: In 2003, after more than a decade of dormancy, the former Erie Railroad main line between Cass Street in Hornell, New York, and Meadville, Pennsylvania, was reactivated as a through route. Local service is provided by a short line called Western New York & Pennsylvania, but the most significant traffic are Norfolk Southern unit coal trains that serve power plants in central New York state. On October 13, 2008, NS loaded train No. 522 is east of Tip Top near Alfred, New York. The train loaded at CONSOL's Loveridge Mine in West Virginia and reached the old Erie via Shire Oaks, Pennsylvania. It was destined for the AES Greenridge plant at Dresden, New York, on the old New York Central Fall Brook Route. *Brian Solomon*

Left: On August 26, 1988, Bessemer & Lake Erie F7s Nos. 728 and 727 perform switching work at Rosebud Mining's Blacksburg Tipple on the Western Allegheny Division. Originally an isolated branch line owned by the Pennsylvania Railroad, the Western Allegheny was sold to the B&LE in 1967 and operated until November 1994. It was atypical of B&LE operations, since trains were assigned rebuilt F7s instead of six-motor road switchers. It primarily served online coal tipples that processed locally strip-mined coal. *Scott R. Snell*

Above: A Pennsylvania Power & Light unit train poses for a photo shoot on the Clymer Loop on October 7, 2001. This tight horseshoe curve is located on the former Cherry Tree & Dixonville Railroad at Purchase Line, Pennsylvania. The Cherry Tree & Dixonville was jointly owned by the Pennsylvania Railroad and the New York Central, running between its namesake towns in western Pennsylvania. RJ Corman acquired this branch from Conrail in 1995 as part its Clearfield Cluster purchase. *Mark Leppert*

Right: A Pennsylvania Power & Light unit train loads on Conrail at the Greenwich Collieries load-out on the former Pennsylvania Railroad Susquehanna Extension Branch at Kinport, Pennsylvania, on March 10, 1990. The train is destined to the Montour Steam Electric Station at Strawberry Ridge, Pennsylvania, on the Washingtonville Secondary near Danville. Pennsylvania Power & Light was an early pioneer in unit train service, and their hoppers can be identified by their PPLX reporting marks. *Mike Harting*

Clean Air Act

The primary impetus for more stringent air-pollution controls in the United States occurred as a result of an incident in October 1948, when an atmospheric inversion in the Monongahela River Valley trapped smoke laden with sulfur dioxide (SO_2) and zinc dust for five days over the town of Donora, Pennsylvania. Twenty people died from asphyxiation, and another 7,000 of the town's 14,000 residents became ill. The Donora tragedy and other air-quality problems prompted the federal government to examine air pollution, which resulted in the enactment of the Air Pollution Control Act of 1955. Further legislation the 1960s set limits for stationary and mobile emission sources.

Despite these early actions, the legislation was seen as inadequate, and in the 1960s, Senator Edmund Muskie of Maine held congressional hearings on air pollution that brought about the Clean Air Act (CAA) of 1970. The same year, Congress created the Environmental Protection Agency (EPA) to administer the provisions of the new laws. One of the principal parts of the act established National Ambient Air Quality Standards (NAAQS), which required the EPA to identify and set standards for six known pollutants: carbon monoxide (CO), nitrogen dioxide (NOx), ozone (O_3), sulfur dioxide (SO_2), particulate matter less than or equal to 10 microns in size (PM-10), and lead (Pb). During the following decade, amendments and revisions extended deadlines imposed by the original act.

Although there were no new amendments in the 1980s, Americans became more environmentally conscious, and acid rain became a gauging mark for environmental damage. Acid rain describes higher than natural amounts of sulfur and nitrogen oxides in rainwater. This occurs when sulfur and nitrogen compounds present in fossil fuels are combusted or oxidized, forming compounds that react with rainwater to form weak acids. When SO_2 and NOx are released from power plants and other sources, prevailing winds can blow these compounds for hundreds of miles, sometimes crossing state and national borders.

Growing concerns over acid rain and other environmental issues resulted in the Clean Air Act Amendments of 1990, which included the first attempt at specific emissions reductions in an effort to curb acid rain. This established a market-based program called "cap and trade" aimed at lowering harmful emissions. This capped SO_2 emissions at approximately half the 1990 levels to be implemented by 1995, thus affecting any fossil fuel–burning electric-generating unit or EGU with capacity to produce 25 megawatts or more. To quantify the rate of pollution, the EPA gave all the affected plants a share of capped emission levels in the form of acid rain permits or "allowances." These were handed out like environmental playing cards for the big polluters and implemented in incrementally more stringent phases. The first compliance phase was in 1995, the second phase in 2000.

The market-based trading program did not make specific requirements for how individual facilities should comply with the new rules, only that each submit an allowance for each ton of SO_2 emitted in a year. Affected polluting facilities must also completely and accurately measure and report

(continued)

to clear the car dumper. Initially, the trains operated with a pair SD40-2s and a GP38-2; by the early 1990s, when the PP&L trains began loading on the former Monongahela Railway, they were assigned three SD40-2s. As a result of the Conrail split, CSX ended up with part of the Strawberry Ridge units. NS's shortage of locomotives that conformed with the working dimensions of the car dumper resulted in trains loading on the former Monongahela Railway with standard NS road units and changing to Strawberry Ridge units at either Altoona or Lock Haven, Pennsylvania, for the remainder of the run to the plant. This kept a handful of Conrail-painted SD40-2s in captive service for a few years. As of 2008, NS assigned 21 former Conrail SD60Is (Nos. 6717–6737) in three-unit sets on the PP&L trains.

Other New Traffic Patterns

The Conrail split has changed routing patterns for coal moving to a variety of significant customers. This has provided mining companies, electric utilities, and steel mills new options for coal. Prior to the split, mines shipping coal for export on Conrail lines were largely limited to moving coal through the CONSOL Energy Terminal in Baltimore and via Ashtabula Harbor on Lake Erie. Since the split, mines on former Conrail lines also have access to Virginia's Hampton Roads tidewater ports, specifically Norfolk Southern's Lambert Point facilities and the former Chesapeake & Ohio facilities at Newport News (now operated by Dominion Terminal), as well as the Kinder Morgan Pier IX facility, also at Newport News.

Among changes on CSX's former Baltimore & Ohio—where, in seemingly incongruous moves, loaded coal trains destined for different customers pass one another between Connellsville and New Castle, Pennsylvania—are the routes that trains take. Some coal loaded on the former Monongahela Railway that formerly used old B&O West End—known more recently as CSX's Mountain Sub—now moves east to Baltimore over the former B&O Sand Patch Grade.

Clean Air Act, continued...

all emissions in a timely manner to the EPA in order to guarantee that an overall cap on emission is achieved.

Power plants affected by new requirements were given several options to comply. Because requirements were not specific to individual polluting facilities, plants affected were able to purchase pollution credits, called "excess allowances," from facilities that had already reduced emissions to below the accepted compliance levels. However, for a power plant to actually reduce its SO_2 emission level it had two primary options: install pollution-control equipment known as "scrubbers" that extract harmful SO_2 gas before it is emitted to the atmosphere, or switch to fuel that would emit less SO_2.

It was this element of the restriction that affected the type of coal on the market because it gave low-sulfur fuels a distinct cost advan-tage. Switching fuel was generally the most cost-effective compliance strategy. To do this, many power plants switched from high-sulfur coal that originated at Appalachian and Illinois Basin mines to lower-sulfur coal mined in the Powder River and Uintah basins. This strategy actually reduced SO_2 emissions to levels greater than originally projected. American railroads, which increased their transport capacity to move much greater volumes of low-sulfur PRB coal to power plants across the country, have helped to clean up the environment.

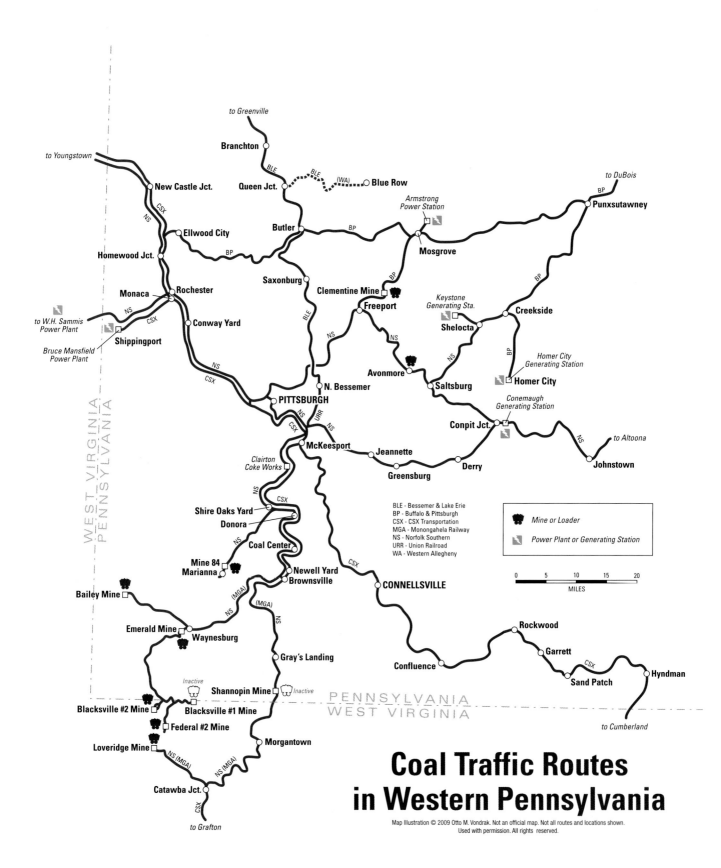

Coal Traffic Routes
in Western Pennsylvania

Map Illustration © 2009 Otto M. Vondrak. Not an official map. Not all routes and locations shown.
Used with permission. All rights reserved.

When CSX took over the former Conrail lines in New York state, the Somerset Generating Station near Lockport received a new routing. Trains loading on the former Monongahela Railway now are interchanged to CSX at Newell, Pennsylvania, and proceed northward along the east side of the Monongahela River Valley to McKeesport, Pennsylvania, where they join the former B&O main line to Chicago. After a crew change at New Castle, Pennsylvania, the train heads west to Center Street Junction in Youngstown, Ohio, where it turns north on the NS Youngstown Line to Ashtabula, Ohio. CSX has trackage rights on NS between Youngstown and Ashtabula to forward coal to the docks at Ashtabula Harbor and to forward coal trains destined to First Energy plants on former Conrail lines in the Cleveland area.

Powder River Coal Comes East

During the last decade, low-sulfur Powder River Basin (PRB) coal from Wyoming has been test-marketed to various power plants east of the Mississippi River served by CSX, NS, and other eastern lines. While some PRB coal moves by rail to Ohio River marine terminals for delivery to power plants by barge, other plants have received PRB coal via unit trains on all-rail routes.

In recent years, BNSF has cooperated with various East Coast utilities interested in testing PRB coal. "Test burn" unit trains have run all the way from PRB mines to East Coast utilities, resulting in solid PRB unit trains—complete with BNSF AC-traction diesels working all the way to Public Service of New Hampshire's Merrimack Generating Station at Bow, New Hampshire (on Guilford Pan Am Railway's Boston & Maine), and to AES Somerset Generating Station near Lockport, New York, via CSX. Traditionally, both of these plants have burned coal from mines in western Pennsylvania and West Virginia.

Norfolk Southern No. 656, with GE model ES40DC No. 7555, leads a westbound loaded train at Tarentum, Pennsylvania, on the former Pennsylvania Railroad Conemaugh Line en route to the Ashtabula Harbor coal dock in Ohio. The coal loaded at the Rosebud Mining siding at Avonmore, Pennsylvania, will be transloaded to lake boats for Ontario Power Generation power plants. *Charles Tipton*

"TEST BURN" UNIT TRAINS FROM POWDER RIVER BASIN HAVE RESULTED IN SOLID UNIT TRAINS—COMPLETE WITH BNSF DIESELS— WORKING ALL THE WAY TO NEW HAMPSHIRE.

Southern Company's subsidiary Georgia Power was among the early converts to a blend of eastern and PRB coal in the mid- to late 1990s. Georgia Power has worked with BNSF and Norfolk Southern to deliver PRB unit trains to its mammoth facility known as Plant Scherer (named for Georgia Power's former chairman and CEO Robert W. Scherer) south of Atlanta. This plant has four 880-megawatt units, the first of which came on-line in 1982. Plant Scherer unit trains can be identified by RWSX reporting marks on coal cars. Typically, BNSF interchanges loaded trains with NS at Memphis, Tennessee.

Above: On September 28, 1991, Conrail SD45-2 No. 6657 leads an empty Somerset coal train (Conrail symbol UNS-39A) out of Seneca Yard at CP5 in Lackawanna, New York, on the former New York Central Water Level Route. Empty Somerset trains were inspected by the Conrail car department at Seneca Yard prior to returning to southwestern Pennsylvania for reloading. *Robert R. Rohauer*

Right: During the winter of 2005–2006, Providence & Worcester teamed up with the New England Central, the Vermont Railway System, and the Canadian Pacific to move 40,000 tons of Indonesian coal from the port of Providence, Rhode Island, to AES Corporation's Westover Generating Station in Johnson City, New York. The four railroads provided an alternative routing to Norfolk Southern, which normally handles coal deliveries to Westover. On January 20, 2006, P&W B39-8 No. 3906 leads a loaded train at Delanson, New York, on the Canadian Pacific. *Jim Shaughnessy*

Alabama Power, another Southern Company subsidiary, receives PRB coal for its Plant Miller generating station located along BNSF's former Frisco line at Palos, Alabama. Named for James H. Miller Jr., a former executive with Alabama Power, the 2,640-megawatt Plant Miller has the distinction of being the first commercial destination for BNSF's PRB coal trains to be equipped with electronically controlled pneumatic (ECP) brakes.

Eastern railroads have sought ways to better serve electric utilities on their lines. For example, Jerry Nassar, leader of Norfolk Southern's resource development team, has looked for means to offer electric utilities cost-alternative all-rail delivery to plants that in recent years have received coal via barge. First Energy—operating former Ohio Edison, Penn Power, Cleveland Electric Illuminating, and Toledo Edison generating stations—was one of

In the early 1980s New York State Electric & Gas constructed the new 684-megawatt Somerset Generating Station on the southern shore of Lake Ontario. Somerset typically burns 5,000 tons of coal daily, primarily northern Appalachian coal from mines located along the former Monongahela Railway. Somerset was built with a flue gas desulfurization (FGD) system to remove excess SO_2 from the flue gas. During the summer months, unit stone trains deliver limestone required by the FGD system. On March 3, 1992, Conrail Somerset coal train (symbol UNS-60A) unloads at the station. *Robert R. Rohauer*

the first to avail themselves of the new NS service arrangements. While First Energy's former CEI and Toledo Edison generating stations have received unit coal trains since the Conrail era, its former Ohio Edison and Penn Power plants, located along the Ohio River at Stratton and Shadyside, Ohio, have burned coal delivered by barge or truck from local strip mines. Based in Pittsburgh, Nassar's department worked with First Energy to build a new siding and unloading pit to dump Rapid Discharge hopper cars at its Sammis plant located along the former PRR line at Stratton, Ohio, between Rochester, Pennsylvania, and Powhattan Point, Ohio. Now Sammis receives daily unit trains of PRB coal interchanged with BNSF near the Chicago gateway in Cicero, Illinois. In 2004, Sammis had the distinction of receiving the billionth ton of coal loaded at Arch Coal's Black Thunder Mine in Wyoming.

CSX also serves First Energy power plants, including the former Penn Power Bruce Mansfield plant in Shippingport, Pennsylvania (northwest of Pittsburgh). A new loop track and unloading pit enables the rapid unloading of unit trains. This plant is at the end of the former Pittsburgh & Lake Erie Kobuta Branch now served by CSX. (Ironically, Shippingport was the location of the

Above: A Pittsburgh & Lake Erie coal train destined for Bow, New Hampshire, approaches Tifft Street in Buffalo, New York, in April 1988. About the time of the Conrail merger, P&LE gained trackage rights over the former Nickel Plate Road between Ashtabula, Ohio, and Buffalo to make a connection with Delaware & Hudson for its unit trains. (D&H reached Buffalo via trackage rights on Conrail's former route.) Coal trains to New England would routinely run through with P&LE locomotives. These trains used a Delaware & Hudson/Boston & Maine routing to reach New Hampshire Public Service's Merrimack generating station in Bow, New Hampshire. Other trains for Bow used a Conrail routing to Rotterdam Junction for interchange with B&M. *Don Rohauer*

Right: In the harsh winter climates of the Midwest and Northeast, rotary car dumpers are protected in purpose-built shelters, which are often preceded by thaw sheds that warm frozen coal. Only radiant heat may be used to thaw aluminum cars. To aid in thawing and dumping, mines apply a freeze-proofing agent during loading. *Patrick Yough*

A friendly wave is reciprocated. In June 1989, Springfield Terminal SD26 No. 639 leads westbound empties from the Bow, New Hampshire, power plant and past the old passenger station at Eagle Bridge, New York, on the Boston & Maine main line. This empty train continued to Rotterdam Junction (west of Albany, New York), where it was interchanged with Conrail. Although this B&M line has seen Bow trains for decades, over the years, Bow coal trains have originated at many different mines and used a variety of routes to reach New England. *Brian Solomon*

first nuclear reactor built to generate commercial electric power.)

At Monaca, Pennsylvania, across the river from the NS's massive Conway Yard, is Colona Transfer Company's marine transfer facility served by CSX's former Pittsburgh & Lake Erie main line. CSX delivers nearly daily PRB unit trains, which it receives from BNSF at Cicero, Illinois. These trains often use BNSF locomotives. Colona also transloads bituminous unit trains loaded on CSX and metallurgical coal originating on CSX spinoff Buffalo & Pittsburgh that is destined for the Mountain States Carbon coke plant in Follansbee, West Virginia.

Norfolk Southern Enters a New Era

Although distributed power units (DPUs)—the modern term for remote-controlled diesel locomotives—have been used since the 1960s, Norfolk Southern relied on traditional manned helpers until September 2008. In order to increase route capacity, NS began assigning DPU-equipped, GE-built ES40DCs to coal trains working on former Virginian grades. Traditionally, three individual manned helpers were used to lift unit trains from Alloy, West Virginia, to Spencer, North Carolina, but by assigning DPUs to this route, NS found it could save the cost of two helper crews

Opposite: Norfolk Southern prefers the former Virginian route east of Roanoke for eastbound tonnage trains because it follows the descending grade of the Roanoke River. The massive, tower-supported plate-girder bridge at Stewartsville, Virginia, supports the railroad over the confluence of Falling Creek and the Roanoke River. On November 10, 2006, this trestle carried loaded NS coal train 762, led by NS GE Evolution-series ES40DC No. 7586. Symbol 762 moves coal from West Virginia to the Progress Energy generating station at Hyco, North Carolina. *T. S. Hoover*

Above: A westbound Norfolk Southern empty hopper train has just exited the Natural Tunnel and crosses Bootleg Trestle. It is climbing a 1.7 percent grade and will crest in about 3 miles at Sunbright, Virginia. Scott County, Virginia, was a dry county, and the Bootleg Trestle got its name from an old store nearby that sold illegal bootleg whiskey. *Ron Flanary*

while increasing track capacity by eliminating the need for helpers to return downgrade.

Also in 2008, Norfolk Southern purchased its first modern AC-traction diesels from General Electric. In September, NS ordered 24 ES44AC locomotives from General Electric (Nos. 8000–8023). These were built with new tractive effort performance features that make them ideally suited for slow-speed, heavy-coal service. Shortly after delivery, the railroad assigned two new ES44ACs to Pocahontas Division helper services, replacing three older DC-traction diesels in equivalent service. Previous to the ES44ACs, the only AC-traction locomotives on the NS system were 17 5,000-horsepower Electro-Motive SD80MACs (Nos.

7200–7216) inherited from Conrail. The SD80MACs are understood to have had a problematic history and have spent the majority of their time working in former Conrail territory, typically on coal trains between Pittsburgh and Baltimore and in the South Fork area west of Altoona, Pennsylvania.

Most significant of NS's technological developments occurred on October 11, 2007, when the railroad became the first in the United States to operate a freight train in regular revenue service equipped with ECP brakes (and, for that matter, the first revenue ECP coal train). The pioneering move was a loaded hopper train from the Emerald Mine in Waynesburg, Pennsylvania (on the former Monongahela Railway), destined for the Keystone

At Garwood, West Virginia, on October 30, 2008, Norfolk Southern ES40DC No. 7711 leads symbol coal train 72Q up the nearly 2 percent Clarks Gap Grade on the former Virginian Railway. This coal train operated with remote-controlled, distributed power–equipped GE ES40DC at the rear end, which remained in consist for the length of the trip. In addition to the DPUs, a two-unit ES44AC helper on the rear assists from Alloy, West Virginia, to the summit of the Clarks Gap. The catenary supports on this bridge are a vestige of the Virginian's AC electrification, discontinued by N&W in 1962. *T. S. Hoover*

Generating Station in Shelocta, Pennsylvania (at the end of the newly constructed Keystone Branch). Norfolk Southern's ES40DCs 7660, 7664, and 7665 moved the train of 115 loads. In an interview with William C. Vantuono in *Railway Age*, NS superintendent of air brakes Jamie L. Williams explains, "ECP represents a whole different way of operating.... Our train crews love ECP."

ECP offers a distinct evolutionary improvement over conventional Westinghouse automatic air brakes.

Instead of using changes in train-line air pressure to apply and release brakes, ECP uses an electric signal to actuate air reservoirs on each car. The difference is that ECP applies and releases air brakes significantly quicker and sets the brakes on all the cars simultaneously, where automatic air brakes experience a delay from front to back as the change in air pressure passes though the train line from car to car. As a result, ECP-equipped trains can stop 50 percent more efficiently than a comparable conventional air-brake-equipped train. Notably, ECP provides improved braking characteristics on trains with distributed power on the rear because the train line is charged from both ends of the train at the same time. Other advantages include reduced brake-shoe and wheel wear, improved fuel consumption, improved running times, and, of course, improved safety.

To make full use of cost advantages offered by ECP-equipped trains, air brake rules need to be reworked to allow ECP trains to travel up to 3,500

An old concept is made new. On October 13, 2008, two-week-old Norfolk Southern ES44ACs Nos. 8010 and 8013 work as pushers on a loaded unit train bound for one of Progress Energy's power plants in North Carolina. These diesels feature state-of-the-art three-phase AC traction and work the former N&W Elkhorn Grade at Keystone, West Virginia, where it has been nearly six decades since N&W discontinued its pioneering overhead AC electrification and three-phase jackshaft electrics. *T. S. Hoover*

miles between inspections instead of the 1,000–1,500 miles presently required by the FRA for air-brake-equipped trains. Since each inspection may take up to three hours to complete, fewer inspections will afford considerable time savings and allow quicker cycle times for unit trains.

As of November 2008, Norfolk Southern had assigned ECP-equipped unit coal trains in three distinct services and had two complete ECP-equipped train-sets of 115 rotary gondolas in service between mines on the former Monongahela Railway and the Keystone Generating Station in western Pennsylvania.

Another two sets of 100 Trinity-built, ECP-equipped Rapid Discharge hoppers were operating between mines in the Norton, Virginia, area and Dominion's Clover Power Station at South Boston, Virginia (approximately 100 miles southeast of Roanoke

TRAINS WITH ELECTRONICALLY CONTROLLED PNEUMATIC BRAKES COULD ONE DAY TRAVEL UP TO 3,500 MILES BETWEEN INSPECTIONS INSTEAD OF THE 1,000–1,500 MILES REQUIRED FOR CONVENTIONAL AIR-BRAKE-EQUIPPED TRAINS.

on the former N&W). These trains run with DPUs over a heavily graded route; it has been found that DPUs improve efficiency sufficiently to cut a day from the cycle time.

The third route involves trains that load at mines in the Williamson, West Virginia, area for delivery of coal to Duke Energy plants at Eden and Spencer, North Carolina. These use a pair of trainsets, each consisting of 85 Rapid Discharge cars.

NS's ECP trains require specifically equipped locomotives. The company has outfitted a fleet of 30 General Electric ES40DCs with ECP controls, 6 of which are also set up to operate as DPUs. Another 50 ES40DC locomotives have been provisionally equipped, meaning each locomotive has wiring necessary to carry the ECP signal but does not have ECP brake controls, so these must be used only as trailing units.

Chapter 4
ILLINOIS BASIN COAL

Union Pacific southbound empty coal trains returning to the coalfields from the Union Electric power plant at Labadie, Missouri, await crews on the former Missouri Pacific at Cahokia, Illinois, on December 1, 1985. *Scott Muskopf*

The Illinois Basin covers an area of western Kentucky, southern Indiana, and southern Illinois rich with high-yield but high-sulfur coal. Traditionally, this was a source of intensive traffic for the region's traditional railroads: Illinois Central; Gulf, Mobile & Ohio; Chicago, Burlington & Quincy; Chicago & Eastern Illinois; Missouri Pacific; Milwaukee Road; Monon; New York Central; and Pennsylvania Railroad. In 1974, 26.6 million tons originated in Illinois and 32.5 million tons in Indiana.

Changes imposed by the Clean Air Act and other legislation have greatly reduced demand for this coal, and once-intensive mining areas have been reduced to a shadow of former activity. However, in recent years the high yield afforded by Illinois Basin coal, combined with installation of scrubber technology, has resulted in a nominal resurgence of railroad activity in the region.

Because the area is well connected by inland waterways, much of the coal mined there has traditionally been transported by barges. Today, Class 1 carriers like Canadian National, BNSF, and Union Pacific, as well as a variety of short line and regional railroads, continue to ship Illinois Basin coal to marine reloads, as well as via all-rail moves to generating stations.

Illinois Central and Canadian National

One of the oldest names in American railroading, Illinois Central was often associated with its one-time counsel, Abe Lincoln, and legendary high-rolling engineer, Casey Jones. The railroad's traditional diamond-shaped logo reflected its role as a coal-hauler. In the 1890s, IC greatly expanded its mileage in southern Illinois and aggressively developed the region's soft bituminous coalfields. In *History of the Illinois Central Railroad*, John F. Stover explains that in the two decades prior to World War I, IC increased its coal haulage sixfold, with its annual coal tonnage rising from 1.8 million tons in 1890 to approximately 11.2 million tons in 1910. By that

Above: A southbound Illinois Central Gulf empty coal train passes Gilman, Illinois, on July 15, 1980. The coalfields of southern Illinois provided a major traffic source for ICG predecessor Illinois Central, which hauled millions of tons of this high-sulfur coal to steel mills and utilities in the Chicago area. Some southern Illinois coal was transloaded at Chicago into water vessels for furtherance to customers located along the Great Lakes. This train consists of standard AAR-designed steel three-bay hoppers. *John Leopard*

Right: Canadian National engineer Kyle Fulling waves from the cab of Illinois Central SD70 No. 1015 at Delavan, Illinois. He's working 100 cars of Illinois coal—known on the railroad as a Cedar Rapids coal train—to an interchange at Peoria with Iowa Interstate, which will deliver it to the Archer Daniels Midland plant at Cedar Rapids, Iowa. The train loaded at Freeman United Coal Mining Company's Crown III Mine in Farmersville, Illinois, the last surviving mine in central Illinois. *Steve Smedley*

Illinois Central's Farmersville coal loads are northeast of Springfield, Illinois, and accelerating away from a slow order behind Illinois Central SD70 No. 1027. The train loaded at the Crown III Mine and is bound for the Archer Daniels Midland plant at Decatur. *Steve Smedley*

time coal represented 34 percent of the railroad's total freight tonnage. Not all of IC's coal came from southern Illinois, however. R. E. Barr, writing for the railroad in its self-published *Organization and Traffic of the Illinois Central System*, points out that in 1937, Illinois mines generated roughly 60 percent of IC's coal traffic, while 35 percent came from mines in western Kentucky (the remainder was produced in Indiana and Alabama). At that time, the railroad was moving 15.2 million tons annually.

Long before modern environmental regulations, soft bituminous coal was recognized as noxious compared with harder, cleaner-burning coal from central Appalachia, so even in the 1930s IC moved relatively small volumes of coal for use as heating fuel to the Chicago market, which preferred clean-burning coal from West Virginia and eastern Kentucky. Nevertheless, the market for southern Illinois coal grew rapidly after World War II as a result of increased demand for electricity. Stover noted that by the 1950s coal represented roughly 40 percent of the railroad's tonnage, and in 1955 it carried approximately 32 million tons of coal. In 1963, steam coal for electrical generation accounted for two-thirds of IC's coal business. That year, IC adopted the unit train concept, making it one of the earliest railways to do so.

IN THE TWO DECADES PRIOR TO WORLD WAR I, IC INCREASED ITS COAL HAULAGE SIXFOLD— FROM 1.8 MILLION TONS IN 1890 TO 11.2 MILLION TONS IN 1910.

Led by three new Missouri Pacific C36-7s, a loaded Union Pacific coal train from southern Illinois bound for the Union Electric plant at Labadie, Missouri, enters Grand Avenue interlocking in St. Louis on May 26, 1986. This scene has changed dramatically since the photo was made: the tower has been razed, and the locomotives retired. Construction of a light-rail system has resulted in substantial track infrastructure changes, while Illinois Basin coal has lost out to low-sulfur Powder River coal. *Scott Muskopf*

In 1972, Illinois Central merged with Gulf, Mobile & Ohio, forming Illinois Central Gulf. During the 1970s and 1980s, ICG trimmed its network through route abandonment and line sales. Among former IC routes sold off were the once-busy coal lines in western Kentucky, which in 1988 formed a new regional railroad called Paducah & Louisville.

In 1998, the pared-down ICG network readopted the Illinois Central name and old black-and-white livery for its locomotives. IC was an anomaly in American railroading—where the bulk of traffic flowed east–west, IC continued to move in its traditional north–south axis, even as surrounding railroads had merged to form ever-larger east–west networks.

In one of the final railroad mergers of the 1990s, the recently privatized Canadian National swallowed up IC. IC's patterns of coal movement in southern Illinois had greatly changed since its heyday. Many of the mines in the region had closed. In some

Above: In a photo staged by Pioneer Railcorp, three Peoria & Western Railway GP20Rs pose on a unit coal train with the Duck Creek power station looming in the background. P&W delivers coal to Ameren Energy Resources' Duck Creek station south of Canton, Illinois, by way of a new 2-mile spur built by Ameren specifically to reach the plant. *Steve Smedley*

Left: An empty Union Pacific coal train leaves UP's Chester Subdivision in East St. Louis, Illinois, crossing the Mississippi River on Terminal Railroad Association (TRRA) trackage over the MacArthur Bridge. These empties will continue west on TRRA to Grand Avenue, where TRRA joins the Jefferson City Subdivision (former Sedalia Subdivision). This route has experienced rapid coal traffic growth during the last 20 years as a result of the increasing volume of Powder River coal moving east through the St. Louis gateway. *Marshall W. Beecher*

cases the coal had tapped out, but in many situations the deciding factor in mine closure was the coal's high sulfur content, deemed too costly to burn after the Clean Air Act. Yet, the region's coal also has one of the highest thermal contents of any coal in North America, which makes it attractive to power plants because less coal needs to be burned to produce the same amount of heat for generation of electricity. With the advent of flue gas desulphurization systems, or "scrubbers," and the rising cost of transport, locally mined coal became more attractive and once again began flowing in greater volumes. In 2008, CN was serving three large mines in southern and central Illinois and delivering their product to a variety of destinations.

Galatia Load-Out

Located in Saline County near the village of Galatia on a branch extending off the Edgewood Cutoff (now CN's Bluford Subdivision) from Ferber, the Galatia load-out serves two underground mines operated by American Coal Company (part of Murray Energy Corporation) and is the second largest supplier of coal on CN's U.S. lines. Coal from the New Future No. 5 Mine and the New Era Mine is loaded at this facility. As of 2008, it typically generated 40 trains per month. It is served by a loop track making a complete circle to speed the loading process. Galatia-loaded trains vary in length depending on their destination, but 100- to 105-car trains are normal. Galatia trains supply a variety of destinations, mostly marine reloading points for further shipment by barge or ship. In the past, the facility has loaded CN trains destined for Archer Daniels Midland in Decatur, Illinois, and for a power plant at Somerset, Kentucky, through an interchange with Norfolk Southern in Centralia, Illinois.

Pond Creek Mine

Located in northeastern Williamson County at Dial near Marion, Illinois, Williamson Energy opened Pond Creek Mine in 2006. It taps a seam of bituminous steam coal used exclusively by power plants. A new branch built to reach the mine is served solely by CN. In 2008, Pond Creek originated approximately 47 monthly unit trains. The majority of these delivered coal to Ohio and Tennessee river transloads and transloads at Mound City, Illinois, and Convent, Louisiana. Approximately one train a month runs to the KCBX Terminal in Chicago, with other moves going to the Archer Daniels Midland plant at Decatur, Illinois, and to the C. Reiss Coal Company docks at Green Bay, Wisconsin.

Coal Past and Future

The impermanent nature of coal mining has resulted in numerous changes in the source of southern Illinois coal over the years. In just the last decade, a number of once-significant mines have closed and new ones developed.

Many of the electric power plants that previously burned southern Illinois coal have largely switched to western coal in recent decades. In a few instances, changes in market conditions have resulted in closed mines being temporarily reopened and served by CN before being closed again.

One of the most significant mines in the region had been the famous Captain and Kathleen Mine (often known as just the Captain Mine). In the 1960s this mine generated up to two trains a day for Gulf, Mobile & Ohio (later Illinois Central Gulf). Although the mine was closed in 1999, between November 23, 2005, and November 6, 2006, 13 unit trains carried coal from the tipple at the mine. Some of the coal originated from stockpiles, while some was also trucked from smaller nearby mines without rail access. Since 2006, there has been no significant activity at this facility.

Rend Lake Mine was served by a CN branch that left the Charter Line (IC's original main line), now the Centralia Subdivision, at Bois, Illinois. The last CN train departed Rend Lake on June 28, 2002, for Mound City, although Union Pacific continued to serve the mine a little longer.

Liberty Mine (once known as Brushy Creek Mine) was reopened in August 2002 and closed

New Illinois Central SD70s charge northbound through Tilden, Illinois, on July 11, 1996, with coal from CONSOL Energy's Rend Lake Mine near Sesser, Illinois. The IC crew remained with the train through Gateway Western Railway's East St. Louis Yard and onto Terminal Railroad Association and joint Southern Pacific/Gateway Western trackage to reach Reuters Siding on the Norfolk Southern. Later, an NS crew delivered the train to the Federal Power Plant in Alton, Illinois. *Scott Muskopf*

again after the final shipment four years later. The track remains at this facility and is currently used for staging empty trains waiting to load at the nearby Pond Creek and Galatia mines. In addition to mines served by CN via former IC routes were a host of mines tapped by Missouri Pacific and Chicago, Burlington & Quincy (later BN). These mines have long since closed.

Sugar Camp Energy is constructing a large new underground mine at Akin Junction (on the former IC Edgewood Cutoff). Sugar Camp Mine No. 1 is expected to open in 2009, and it is hoped it will produce between 40 and 45 unit trains per month for CN. Meanwhile, the Galatia mines, which have been two of the largest producers of coal for CN in Illinois, are expected to load fewer trains in the next few years.

Yankeetown Dock Corporation SD38-2s lead southbound coal loads at Yankeetown, Indiana, on October 26, 1994. The coal, from a nearby mine at Boonville, was headed either for the Warwick power plant or the barge facility on the Ohio River. *John Leopard*

Transloading Destinations

Many CN unit trains convey coal to marine terminals for final delivery by barge or ship. Among these are two significant Gulf Coast transloading points. The McDuffie Coal Terminal, located at the port of Mobile, Alabama, transloads coal to barges for domestic transport to myriad power plants along the Gulf Coast and Intracoastal Waterway. This facility is located at the terminus of CN's Beaumont Subdivision from Jackson, Mississippi, and it receives roughly seven CN trains a month. By contrast, CN's IC Rail-Marine Terminal at Convent, Louisiana, northwest of New Orleans on the Mississippi River,

primarily handles coal bought by brokers and resold to customers in Europe and South America.

Many of the region's coal trains have relatively short hauls to transloads at Calvert City Terminal at Calvert, Kentucky, on the Tennessee River; the Grand River Terminal at Jessup, Kentucky, on the Tennessee River; and Cook Terminal on the Ohio River at Metropolis, Illinois. Coal transloaded to barges at these points is destined for power plants along the Ohio and Tennessee river systems.

Both Calvert City and the Grand River Terminal are well situated for moving coal via the Tennessee Valley Authority inland waterway network. In addition to southern Illinois coal moved by CN, the Calvert City facility serves Powder River Basin unit trains operated by Union Pacific and BNSF. Although the facility has staging tracks up to 7,500 feet long, these are generally reserved for standard-

A southbound empty Union Pacific coal train, powered by Illinois Central Gulf SD40-2s, awaits a crew on the siding at Cahokia, Illinois, on April 18, 1987. Contracts between Kerr-McGee Coal, Union Electric, UP, and Illinois Central Gulf resulted in dedicated coal hopper and locomotive pools operating from mines in southern Illinois (on former Missouri Pacific and Illinois Central lines) to Union Electric power plants in eastern Missouri served by UP and Burlington Northern. *Scott Muskopf*

length PRB coal trains, relegating CN's trains to shorter 6,500-foot staging tracks. These trains are limited to 105 cars. Reaching the Cook facility is awkward for CN unit trains and requires a 5-mile reverse move over BNSF between Metropolis, Illinois, and the terminal. Typically, trains carry a caboose to aid in this maneuver.

In 2008, three to four CN trains per month from Galatia served the Cahokia Marine Terminal at Sauget, near East St. Louis, which receives the bulk of its coal from the PRB via BNSF and UP. This terminal supplies coal to various power plants along the Mississippi River. CN also has access to the Consolidated Grain & Barge Company transload at Mound City, Illinois, on the Ohio River.

Operations

Compared with the monster trains now operated out of the Powder River Basin and on some eastern lines, CN coal trains are more conservative in size, with many trains in the 90- to 105-car range. Since the territory is largely level, train size is not governed so much by grades but by other practical considerations. For example, CN's typical loaded 105-car train of aluminum hoppers weighs approximately 14,000 tons and is normally assigned just two modern 4,000- to 4,400-horsepower diesels, typically Electro-Motive Division's SD70, SD70i, and SD75i, or General Electric's Dash 9s. (In IC days, standard coal power comprised three SD40-2s.) If the train was any heavier, it would require three modern

In was raining on April 13, 2008, when CSX coal train V502 crossed the Wabash River bridge on the former Baltimore & Ohio at Vincennes, Indiana. Earlier in day, the train had loaded at Black Beauty Coal Mining's load-out at Wheatland, Indiana, 12 miles to the east on the former B&O Baltimore–St. Louis main line. The coal is destined to Duke Energy Cayuga Station 90 miles north of Vincennes, Indiana, on CSX's former Chicago & Eastern Illinois Chicago–Nashville main line. In late 2008, the Wheatland load-out was the only location in southern Indiana where coal was loaded along the old B&O main line. *Sean Robitaille*

diesels. Running 25 to 30 additional cars per train would not take sufficient advantage of the additional locomotive to justify the cost of assigning it. One exception is any unit train loaded at Pond Creek for Mound City. These require three locomotives because of the "Charter Line" grades they cross in the Illinois Ozarks south of Carbondale. Other considerations affecting train length are the size of load-outs and yards that were built to smaller standards.

Looking at CN's coal trains in the United States at midday on October 7, 2008, there were 12 loaded and empty CN trains on the railroad, plus one additional empty set off-line but returning to CN for reloading. The smallest of these trains was a C78591-07 with 74 CN (former IC) cars passing Effingham, Illinois,

destined for C. Reiss at Green Bay, Wisconsin. The largest was a 115-car train of GEAX cars from Pond Creek unloading at Convent, Louisiana.

Among the more interesting moves are trains loaded at Galatia and interchanged at Paducah, Kentucky, with Paducah & Louisville for delivery to the Grand River and Calvert City terminals. These trains make the whole run using CN locomotives and complete a loading cycle from mine to plant and back in 54 hours (including 36 hours on the P&L). CN also interchanges about four trains monthly to CSX via the P&L for shipment to the Tennessee Valley Authority Widows Creek Fossil Plant at Bridgeport, Alabama. These trains run with CSX locomotives over the length of their cycle.

Indiana Railroad (INRD) has developed a considerable short-haul operation for coal between both online and offline mines and power plants in southern Indiana. On April 15, 2008, an empty Merom dumper train powered by INRD's SD40-2 fleet grinds to a halt just west of Linton, Indiana. Earlier, the train dumped coal at Indianapolis Power & Light's Merom power plant near New Lebanon, Indiana, and it is now heading east for interchange with the Indiana Southern Railroad for a trip back to the mines south of Petersburg, Indiana. *Sean Robitaille*

Indiana Southern (ISRR) operates short-haul coal trains on its former New York Central and Pennsylvania Railroad trackage between Indianapolis and Evansville, Indiana. Most of the coal is delivered to Indianapolis Power & Light plants. In the late morning of April 15, 2008, an ISRR train pulls through the load-out at Somerville Mine near Somerville, Indiana. Once loaded, the train will run north and deliver coal to Indianapolis Power & Light's plant at Petersburg, Indiana. *Sean Robitaille*

Chapter 5
POWDER RIVER BASIN COAL

This going-away view of Burlington Northern coal loads at West Caballo Junction, Wyoming, depicts five BN SD40-2s and a fuel tender against a backdrop of the Coal Creek Mine. *C. Richard Neumiller*

The rolling grasslands of central Wyoming and eastern Montana are the antithesis of Appalachian coal country. Where in Appalachia, coal is located in mountains and deep valleys, often wedged between layers of rock, the coal from these windswept high plains—the Powder River Basin—is approximately 100 feet below the grass. Here, compliance coal reserves have been described as the equivalent of three times the energy wealth of the Saudi Arabian oilfields—an estimated 25 billion tons.

Crawling along like gigantic worms and destined for myriad power plants and coal docks across North America, coal trains pulse out of the Powder River Basin on specially built lines. Sixty to seventy loaded trains a day, plus the tide of returning empties, make for a lot of heavy railroad activity. Train weights vary depending on the loading mine and customer requirements but range from 13,400 to more than 18,000 tons. At present, all PRB trains are handled by either BNSF Railway or Union Pacific.

Putting the Powder River coal boom in perspective, consider that back in the 1950s when American railroads were replacing steam locomotives en masse with diesels, Powder River coal wasn't yet a source of railroad traffic. When the last revenue steam locomotive dumped its fire, the tracks through the Powder River Basin didn't even exist. Nothing more than prairie grass grew where today a multiple-track line hosts a diesel-hauled, 135-car coal train every few minutes. Today, PRB coal trains account for some of the heaviest and densest traffic on American railroads, and the jointly run BNSF/UP Orin Cutoff that taps mines in central Wyoming is believed to be the heaviest tonnage freight railroad in North America, if not the world. This is not only modern railroading at its finest—without question it is one of the greatest success stories in American freight railroading.

Since the formative days of the industry, American railroads have had an integral relationship with coal movement. Numerous early lines, including the pioneering Delaware & Hudson and Baltimore & Ohio, owed their development to coal mines situated along their lines. Mines in Pennsylvania, West Virginia, Virginia, Kentucky, and southern Illinois poured forth coal as fast as the railroads could haul it. By contrast, coalfields in Wyoming and eastern Montana had very limited economic value. The combination of relatively low energy yield and both high ash and water content meant the stuff was of little value on the market.

Even if it was deemed desirable, it was uneconomical to mine because it was so far from major markets. Years ago, the old Northern Pacific—a component company of BNSF predecessor Burlington Northern—developed Rosebud coal mines along its lines largely to supply cheap fuel for its own locomotives. The burn quality of Rosebud coal was so low that NP needed to develop special locomotives with extra-large fireboxes to make productive use of this fuel. Its famous Yellowstone articulated locomotives had the largest fireboxes of any steam locomotive ever built—22 feet long and 9 feet wide—big enough to stage a banquet inside one as a publicity stunt.

So what changed? How was Powder River coal transformed from an insignificant source of railroad traffic to one of most the significant in just a few years? The story behind the Power River coal boom involves four essential events: the Burlington Northern merger of 1970, the Clean Air Act of 1970, the Arab oil embargo of 1973, and the Staggers Act of 1980. Subsequent to these events, the dynamic growth in the movement of Powder River coal has been fueled by continued pursuit of cleaner energy, the rising cost of crude oil, and ever-increasing energy demands.

From a historical perspective, it's fascinating how the tide of Powder River coal transformed

AT AN ESTIMATED 25 BILLION TONS, PRB COAL RESERVES HAVE BEEN DESCRIBED AS THE EQUIVALENT OF THREE TIMES THE ENERGY WEALTH OF THE SAUDI ARABIAN OILFIELDS.

COINCIDENT WITH THE FORMATION OF BN WAS THE PASSAGE OF THE 1970 CLEAN AIR ACT— PRB COAL HAS SULFUR CONTENT AS LOW AS 0.2 PERCENT.

the old Hill Lines—those historic railroads closely affiliated with each other since the days of James J. Hill, the genius of early-twentieth-century railroading, known as the "Empire Builder." In 1970, following years of discussions, Chicago, Burlington & Quincy (CB&Q), Northern Pacific (NP), and Great Northern (GN), plus related properties, were merged to form the new Burlington Northern (BN). At that time, none of BN's component railroads were large-scale coal haulers. In *Burlington Northern Railroad: Coal Hauler and Coal Country Trackside Guide*, authors Patrick C. Dorin and Robert C. Del Grosso explain how in the late 1960s GN annually hauled just 2.9 million tons of coal, NP 1.42 million tons, and CB&Q approximately 12 million tons. Of CB&Q's coal traffic, the largest portion was from the southern Illinois coalfields, with only a trickle from Wyoming's Powder River Basin.

In 1970, BN moved just 21.2 million tons of coal system-wide, of which PRB coal represented only 3 to 4 million tons. Although these may seem like large numbers, they are paltry sums compared with production totals today, and even with the major coal lines of the period.

Coincident with the formation of BN was the passage of the 1970 Clean Air Act, which had provisions aimed at reducing SO_2 emissions that had been deemed the cause of acid rain. This seemingly obscure clause was key to the economic value of PRB coal. Previously, coal consumers rarely worried about sulfur content. In the East, much of the easiest coal mined was of high-yield bituminous varieties that also had high sulfur content. By comparison, PRB coal had sulfur content as low as 0.2 percent.

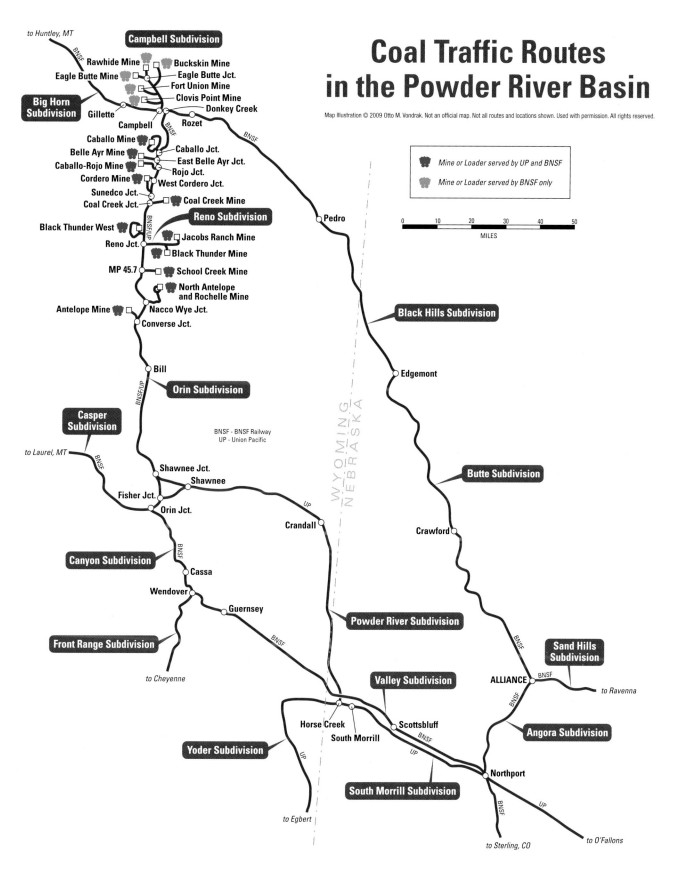

Coal Traffic Routes
in the Powder River Basin

Map Illustration © 2009 Otto M. Vondrak. Not an official map. Not all routes and locations shown. Used with permission. All rights reserved.

to Huntley, MT

Campbell Subdivision

Rawhide Mine
Buckskin Mine
Eagle Butte Mine
Eagle Butte Jct.
Fort Union Mine
Big Horn Subdivision
Clovis Point Mine
Gillette
Donkey Creek
Campbell
Rozet
Caballo Mine
Caballo Jct.
Belle Ayr Mine
East Belle Ayr Jct.
Caballo-Rojo Mine
Rojo Jct.
Cordero Mine
West Cordero Jct.
Sunedco Jct.
Coal Creek Mine
Coal Creek Jct.
Reno Subdivision
Black Thunder West
Jacobs Ranch Mine
Reno Jct.
Black Thunder Mine
MP 45.7
School Creek Mine
North Antelope and Rochelle Mine
Antelope Mine
Nacco Wye Jct.
Converse Jct.

Pedro

Bill

BNSF/UP

Orin Subdivision

Casper Subdivision

to Laurel, MT

BNSF - BNSF Railway
UP - Union Pacific

Shawnee Jct.
Shawnee
Fisher Jct.
Orin Jct.

Crandall

Black Hills Subdivision

Edgemont

Butte Subdivision

Crawford

Canyon Subdivision

Cassa
Wendover

Guernsey

Front Range Subdivision

to Cheyenne

Powder River Subdivision

Valley Subdivision

Sand Hills Subdivision

ALLIANCE
to Ravenna

Angora Subdivision

Horse Creek
Scottsbluff
South Morrill

Yoder Subdivision

Northport

South Morrill Subdivision

to Egbert

to Sterling, CO

to O'Fallons

WYOMING
NEBRASKA

Mine or Loader served by UP and BNSF

Mine or Loader served by BNSF only

0   10   20   30   40   50
MILES

111

BNSF empty train E-CRDJRM1-60 rolls north through South Huntsman, Nebraska, on the Angora Subdivision on September 29, 2008. It will reload at Wyoming's Jacobs Ranch Mine, which is the fourth-largest coal mine in the United States and produced more than 38 million tons of coal in 2007. *Patrick Yough*

Suddenly, the vast tracts of coal beneath windswept Wyoming had value if it could be transported to market economically.

The newly merged BN had the good fortune of possessing routes that crisscrossed the Powder River region. Equally important, the railroad's management had the wisdom and resources to make the most of a fortuitous position. At the time, gloom prevailed over the American railroad industry. The eastern giants stood on the precipice of oblivion, some of the Midwestern railroads were insolvent, and pundits were raising serious questions about the financial viability of railroads across the nation. Against this cloud, the Powder River coal boom emerged as a shining moment of hope.

With budding markets on the horizon, coal companies planned new mines for the PRB during the early 1970s. BN moved to tap this new traffic with an application to the Interstate Commerce Commission (ICC) for construction of a 14-mile branch from Donkey Creek southward to the new AMAX Coal Company's Belle Ayr Mine. Located 12 miles east of Gillette, Donkey Creek is a nondescript spot on the former CB&Q main line from Lincoln via Alliance, Nebraska, to Huntley, Montana (near Billings). Previously, this lightly traveled transcontinental link had never enjoyed heavy traffic volumes. It was a bold move for a railroad to consider new construction at a time when elsewhere lines were being downgraded or abandoned, but BN made news by laying new track.

On September 25, 1997, capacity expansion was under way on the Orin Subdivision at Converse Junction, Wyoming. Former Burlington Northern SD60M No. 9218 leads BNSF unit train C-BTMMLP2-14. *Mike Abalos*

The Belle Ayr Mine was just the beginning. By 1972, BN had already anticipated further growth and submitted to the ICC plans for an entirely new railroad route that would extend the Belle Ayr branch south through the Powder River Basin to a connection with its east–west Wendover–Laurel route east of Orin, Wyoming. This route had a dual purpose: it would cut through the heart of PRB coal territory to tap a host of new mines while also serving as a new strategic route to connect two former CB&Q main lines in the region. Known as the Orin Cutoff, this new line trimmed as much as 155 miles from the path some coal trains would need to travel.

BN was not alone in its interest in PRB coal. The old Chicago & North Western had long served eastern Wyoming via its lightly built Cowboy Line, part of a long-dead scheme by C&NW to push a transcontinental line through to the Pacific. C&NW's Wyoming lines were dead-end branches with paltry amounts of traffic, and C&NW was a financially destitute property. The prospect of intensive coal traffic seemed like a way to inject cash into C&NW's floundering network, so it filed a competing PRB plan with the ICC a year after BN.

At a time when the prevailing philosophy was line consolidation, proposals for construction of new duplicative infrastructure seemed unacceptable to federal regulators. The ICC rejected both BN's and C&NW's petitions. The ICC insisted the railroads

Above: Chicago & North Western Dash 8-40C No. 8530 leads Union Pacific GEs at East Coal Creek Junction in September 1995. Today, coal produces more than half the electricity generated in the United States and is the largest commodity moved by rail. *Scott R. Snell*

Right: Snow falls early in Powder River country. In September 1995, coal trains are queued up head to tail, waiting for authority to proceed. Chicago & North Western No. 8507 waits at a red signal with another loaded train just beyond. *Scott R. Snell*

would need to work together. The ICC approved a jointly financed BN/C&NW plan in January 1976. However, C&NW was unable to finance its half of the new construction, so BN went ahead and built the Orin Cutoff itself. Without question, BN's Orin Cutoff was the most substantial new railroad construction completed in some five decades. The first train rolled off the new line in November 1979.

Infrastructure

In recent times, PRB infrastructure has benefited from modern innovations like heavy alloyed-steel continuous-welded rail, concrete ties, and Centralized Traffic Control. Yet, when BN began its operations in the 1970s, its lines feeding the PRB were largely equipped with older technology. To overcome inadequacies in its physical plant, BN made intensive

Union Pacific No. 5966 leads westbound empties as it passes a loaded train on the former Chicago & North Western at DeKalb, Illinois, on January 23, 2005. *Howard Ande*

infrastructure investment. The Orin Cutoff was built with 132-pound continuous-welded rail on chemically treated wooden ties—3,114 ties per mile—making for an unusually heavy track standard that reflected the anticipated traffic volume. The right-of-way required 26 bridges and used numerous cuts and fills to minimize changes in gradient. An equally important part of BN's coal strategy was upgrading lines that connected with the Orin Cutoff.

Keys to the flow are various former CB&Q routes in the region. Among the lines BN upgraded was its route between Alliance and Gillette via Edgemont, South Dakota. This line traverses Crawford Hill on a sinuous alignment with a 1.55 percent eastward ruling grade. Here, major improvements were necessary to accommodate loaded unit coal trains. Over the grade, BN installed modern two-main track (distinctly different from traditional directional double-track in that trains on two-main track may operate on signal indication over either track in either direction without

regard to conventional traffic restrictions). In addition, BN realigned portions of the line to reduce the severity of curvature, and a short tunnel near Belmont was bypassed in favor of a new deep cutting.

Work began in 1977 and was accomplished concurrently with Orin Cutoff construction. Ultimately, Centralized Traffic Control was installed on virtually all lines feeding the PRB. To minimize bottlenecks, BN installed two-main track at strategic places. It also built 10 new dispatcher-controlled passing sidings on single-track sections. Sidings were tailored to accommodate typical unit coal train lengths (110-car unit trains require passing sidings roughly 8,000 feet long). BN also phased out traditional jointed rail and improved its signal systems on PRB mainline feeders.

Despite its initial investment in infrastructure improvement, BN struggled to cope with ever-increasing demands on its track space as PRB traffic mushroomed in the mid-1970s and early 1980s. By the mid-1980s the railroad was saturated, and operations had begun to congeal. According to Fred Frailey, writing in the November 1989 issue of *Trains* magazine, BN was accommodating 250 unit trainsets on its system; there was so much traffic that the railroad routinely failed to get trains between crew terminals within normal working hours. The efficiency of its PRB operations suffered from traffic burdens. Further investment was needed to restore the efficient flow of coal. By the late 1980s, BN had a handle on its traffic woes, but to keep pace with the demand for coal, it has continued to expand PRB track capacity ever since.

Competition

BN's first full year of operation on the Orin Cutoff contributed greatly to the railroad's coal haulage record: in 1980 it carried more than 105 million tons of coal. Yet, 1980 was significant for far more than just this record, which was soon surpassed. That year,

Congress passed the Staggers Act, crucial legislation that effectively deregulated American railroads. The Staggers Act is often cited as a turning point in modern American railroading and credited with the nationwide revitalization of the industry. It also set the stage for changes that contributed to the growth of PRB coal traffic. Among the key elements of Staggers were fundamental changes allowing railroads to negotiate rates and sign long-term contracts with customers, which had largely been impossible under old rate regulations.

The Staggers Act also opened up the PRB to competition. One side effect of Staggers was a deal designed to quell threatened competition from coal slurry pipelines. In 1980, C&NW had begun working on an arrangement to gain entry into the Powder River. Initially, BN resisted, but the ICC sided with C&NW, so finally in 1983, BN and C&NW worked out a joint ownership agreement involving 93 miles of the Orin Cutoff. This gave C&NW access to key mines along the line, but it needed a modern line to reach the Orin Cutoff.

The Cowboy Line virtually intersected with the Orin Cutoff. In the 1970s, C&NW had considered

KCS train 97 is at Rich Mountain, Arkansas, on October 19, 1986, destined for Gulf States Utilities at Mossville, Louisiana. KCS Nos. 691 and 670 are followed by three BN six-motor GEs. The train was loaded by BN in the Powder River Basin and interchanged to KCS at Kansas City. The 1.5 percent ruling grades on KCS's Rich Mountain Line required manned rear-end helpers on heavy coal trains. *John Leopard*

Above: Two loaded coal trains converge at Converse Junction, Wyoming. The train on the left has just finished loading at the Antelope Mine and will follow the train on the right up Logan Hill, a 7-mile-long 1 percent grade. At the end of 2007, four mainline tracks had been installed through here to handle increasing traffic. *John Leopard*

Left: Kansas City Southern CKCTU26 is a loaded PRB coal train running from the Thunder Basin Coal Company's Coal Creek Mine to Luminant's (formerly Texas Utilities) Monticello steam electric station near Mount Pleasant, Texas. Monticello gets its name from nearby Lake Monticello, a 2,000-acre lake that supplies cooling water to the station. Monticello can burn both locally mined lignite and PRB coal. The cars are a rapid-discharge design known as AutoFlood III built by Freight Car America. *Scott Muskopf*

rebuilding more than 500 miles of the old trans-Nebraska line to tap the PRB. However, the route's lightweight jointed rail and infrequent sidings provided neither the necessary axle-loading to accommodate heavy trains nor the track and siding capacity to move them efficiently. C&NW discarded this option as too costly and instead worked out an arrangement with Union Pacific to accommodate unit coal trains.

117

Chicago Central & Pacific No. 1705 leads a coal load at Blairsburg, Iowa, on October 27, 1994. Chicago Central received unit coal trains from Union Pacific at Council Bluffs, Iowa, for delivery to Commonwealth Edison's power plant in Plaines, Illinois, just south of Chicago. *Mike Abalos*

Under the auspices of a new subsidiary called Western Railroad Properties Incorporated, C&NW constructed an all-new 56-mile route from a UP line at Joyce, Nebraska, to its Cowboy Line at Crandall. It also upgraded (rebuilt with new track, ballast, and bridges) the comparatively short stretch (45 miles) of the old Cowboy between Crandall and Shawnee, Wyoming. At the latter point, it constructed another 6 miles of new line to reach the Orin Cutoff at Shawnee Junction. East of Joyce, C&NW coal trains used the Union Pacific, and at Fallons, Nebraska, this route joined the Union Pacific's heavily built transcontinental main line for movement farther east. C&NW and UP were already partners in the

movement of transcontinental traffic—east of the Missouri River, C&NW's main line had long served as the primary routing for Union Pacific east–west freight traffic.

C&NW built two nominal-sized coal terminals: one at Bill, Wyoming, on the Orin Cutoff, the other east of Joyce at South Morrill, Nebraska. C&NW operated its first PRB coal train in 1984. By the end of the year, it was handling about 11 PRB unit trains daily. C&NW's close relationship with Union Pacific ultimately resulted in UP acquiring the line in 1995. Since then, Union Pacific and BNSF (formed in 1995 as a result of the merger between BN and Santa Fe Railway) have shared traffic originating in the PRB.

Growth

By placing even more stringent restrictions on SO_2 emissions, the Clean Air Act Amendments of 1990 encouraged more utilities to switch to PRB coal. Rising demand saw a dramatic increase in trainloads of PRB coal in the early 1990s. The railroads needed to add capacity to the Orin Cutoff, both to keep operations fluid and to facilitate further growth. First, the Orin Cutoff was equipped with a second main track. As this growth continued, BNSF and UP installed sections of multiple main track. In June 2005, 14 miles of a third main between Walker and Shawnee Junction, Wyoming (where Union Pacific trains diverge to head east), opened for service. An additional 19 miles of the third main was opened for service in September 2006, and

Burlington Northern SD40-2s Nos. 7277, 7110, and 7067 lead westbound coal empties over the Peoria River, Pekin & Union bridge at Peoria, Illinois, on May 3, 1980. *George W. Kowanski*

in 2007, 39 miles of the third main were completed, giving the majority of the Orin Cutoff three main tracks between Donkey Creek Junction and Shawnee Junction. In addition, 14 miles of a fourth main track were installed over Logan Hill on the central portion of the Orin Cutoff. These improvements were designed to allow the railroads to move up to 400 million tons of coal from the PRB per year.

On May 1, 2006, BNSF and Union Pacific set a new joint record by loading 76 trains in the PRB in one day. By the end

THE CLEAN AIR ACT AMENDMENTS OF 1990 INFRASTRUCTURE LED TO IMPROVEMENTS DESIGNED TO ALLOW RAILROADS TO MOVE 400 MILLION TONS OF COAL FROM THE PRB PER YEAR.

A Powder River Basin unit train unloads at the W. A. Parish generating station in Smithers Lake, Texas, on the former Santa Fe line between Houston and Galveston. The Parish plant utilizes two unloading loops with separate rotary car dumpers. An automatic indexing arm moves the train through the car dumper after the BNSF crew spots the first car for unloading. *Patrick Yough*

Twisting eastward through the Sand Hills of Nebraska, train C-BTMSUD0-07 moves coal from Black Thunder Mine to the Superior Midwest Energy Terminal transloading facility at Superior, Wisconsin. To minimize congestion in the Powder River Basin, Superior-bound trains load at mines on the south end of the Powder River Basin and operate via Alliance and Lincoln, Nebraska, while trains loading on the north end of the Basin operate via Glendive, Montana, and Dilworth, Minnesota. *Chris Guss*

A Marion 351M shovel loads a haul truck at Arch Coal's Black Thunder Mine. The haul truck delivers coal to the nearest crusher. From there it is moved via conveyor belt to the loading silo. Haul trucks are supervised by a dispatcher aided by global positioning satellites and MineStar, a program developed by Caterpillar to most effectively route trucks. *Patrick Yough*

of that year, the PRB was considered the heaviest tonnage line in the world. Where Wyoming mines produced an estimated 200 million tons of coal in 1990, BNSF reported in 2007 that Wyoming mines produced 454 million tons of coal, of which 96 percent came from the PRB. Today, 17 mines along the Orin Cutoff produce the lion's share of Wyoming coal traffic for BNSF and Union Pacific. In general, mines have consistently increased production in recent years. According to BNSF, the original Belle Ayr Mine, for example, produced 19.5 million tons in 2005, 24.6 million tons in 2006, and 26.6 million tons in 2007. On average, it can load 7,000 tons of coal an hour.

Black Thunder Mine

One of the most productive mines in the PRB is the Black Thunder Mine, which began shipping coal in December 1977. For years this was the largest coal mine in the United States until Peabody Coal merged the North Antelope Mine with the Rochelle Mine, forming the North Antelope Rochelle Mine complex (NARM). Black Thunder is now operated by the Thunder Basin Coal Company, a subsidiary of Arch Coal Incorporated, which bought the mine from Atlantic Richfield's ARCO Coal subsidiary in 1998. This vast open-pit mine taps the Anderson-Wyodak seam with its average thickness of 68

Union Pacific train CJOBT9-29 starts into the loading loop at the Black Thunder Mine. The train took slightly over an hour to load and departed symbol CBTJO9-03, destined for the Electric Energy plant in Joppa, Illinois. The cars are lettered for Ameren Energy subsidiary Joppa & Eastern Railroad. Ameren is the majority owner in Electric Energy and in 2006 was the largest buyer of Powder River coal. *Patrick Yough*

feet. Typical of the PRB, Black Thunder coal is a low-sulfur, sub-bituminous-grade coal. Arch Coal reported that Black Thunder produced record output in 2006, with 67 million tons; this declined marginally in 2007 to 65 million tons.

Following a PRB Unit Train

Let's follow a Powder River unit train over its cycle. A train must return to PRB empty before it loads, so we'll begin the journey at Chicago with an empty train. At 6:35 a.m. on October 30, 2008, a BNSF crew is on duty at Cicero Yard in the western Chicago suburbs. This is the old Chicago, Burlington & Quincy yard. E-CNRATM9-81 has arrived from Norfolk Southern a few hours earlier. This empty unit train is making the cycle from Detroit Edison's River Rouge plant in Michigan back to the Antelope Mine. The service may use either Norfolk Southern or CSX between Cicero Yard and River Rouge, but we are going to focus on the BNSF portion of the trip.

At 8:29 a.m. E-CNRATM9-81 departs Cicero behind BNSF GE ES44AC No. 5782 and SD70MAC No. 8844 with 128 empty cars. The train is 6,795 feet long and weighs 2,766 tons. It has 3 horsepower per ton—more than ample for getting an empty unit train over the road—but it isn't powered for the empty journey, but rather for the loaded return (the locomotives have to get back west too). The train is allowed a maximum of 55 miles per hour, and unlike the highway traffic that blithely ignores speed limits, the engineers on BNSF will adhere to top speeds as prescribed.

E-CNRATM9-81 runs the length of BNSF's famous "Triple Track" raceway, known for its high volumes of freight and passenger trains. The last of the "dinky rush" (commuters) whizzes past inbound as E-CNRATM9-81 makes its way toward Aurora, which it passes at 9:56 a.m. West of Aurora, BNSF's main lines diverge: the single-track Aurora Sub heads

toward Savanna, Illinois, and La Crosse, Wisconsin, but the empty unit train heads due west on the old CB&Q two-main track Mendota Sub. An hour later it glides through Mendota. Congestion around Galesburg, one of BNSF's busiest hubs, delays the train for almost four hours as traffic with higher priorities is routed through town. E-CNRATM9-81 finally arrives for a crew change at 5:11 p.m. and is rolling west again at 6:28 p.m. At 7:36 p.m. it passes the railroad's namesake—Burlington, Iowa—and arrives at Creston for its next crew change at 2:30 a.m. on Halloween morning. After 11 hours and many miles of prairie-running, our train is at its next crew change in Lincoln, Nebraska. By Halloween night it is at Ravenna, Nebraska, where it changes crews again, leaving Ravenna 12:30 a.m.

Arriving at Alliance, Nebraska, one of BNSF's major Powder River staging yards, at 9:32 a.m. on November 1, E-CNRATM9-81 is due for some adjustments. Its ideal tender—that is the number of coal cars it is expected to load—is 130, yet at Alliance it picks up 4 cars. In addition to the 2 cars it needed to fill out from the 128 with which it departed Chicago is a pair of BNSF 535-series hoppers being repositioned to Guernsey, Wyoming. Also at Alliance, the locomotives are changed to SD70ACe No. 9177, SD70MAC No. 9722, and a DPU locomotive, SD70MAC No. 9807, which is added to the back of the train for the run to the mine. The SD70MACs were designed by Electro-Motive 15 years earlier and were purchased by Burlington Northern, and later BNSF, specifically for heavy-tonnage applications including Powder River unit trains. The DPU isn't needed on the empty train, but it will be required once the train is loaded, and for the time being it helps provide a healthy 4.3 horsepower per ton on 2,854 tons. The empties depart Alliance just before 2 p.m. and make the run to Northport by 3:23 p.m., then on to Guernsey, arriving at 10:25 p.m. The 2 extra cars are set off, and a new crew boards to bring the train to Converse Junction in the Powder River Basin. BNSF's E-CNRATM9-81 arrives at Converse Junction at 5:40 a.m. on November 2. Since the train is running a bit behind schedule, the mine makes efforts to expedite the delivery and loading of the train at Antelope Mine.

Thirteen hours later, the train is back at Converse Junction and ready to head east. It now carries symbol C-ATMCXR0-17, meaning it is a loaded train and will run to River Rouge via a CSX routing east of Chicago. With all 130 cars loaded, the train weighs 18,414 tons and carries 15,604 tons of coal. The consist is just over 6,900 feet long. With 0.6 horsepower per ton, it needs its AC-traction diesels to perform well to make it over the road in good time. Back when BN began operations in the Powder River Basin, five SD40-2s would have been standard power. Three SD70MACs are rated at 12,000 horsepower, versus 15,000 horsepower for the old DC-traction SD40-2s. This train is substantially heavier too. What makes this equation work is the significantly greater tractive effort delivered by the SD70MAC's polyphase AC-traction system.

At 2:35 a.m. on November 3, C-ATMCXR0-17 changes crews at Guernsey. The outbound crew has been on duty since 11:03 p.m., yet despite its late arrival at the mine, the loaded train is now slightly

A steady rain falls in southwest Iowa on September 10, 2006, as a BNSF empty unit train pauses at Creston. After a crew change, the train resumed its westward journey to the Powder River Basin via Lincoln, Nebraska. *Chris Guss*

ahead of its schedule. Two additional locomotives are added here—SD70MAC No. 8944 and SD70ACe No. 9366—for the climb over Angora Hill out of Northport. The loaded train continues eastward on the same route the empties came out on, changing crews at Alliance at 6:15 that evening. At Alliance, the four head-end locomotives are exchanged for SD70MACs Nos. 8972 and 9863, while the DPU, No. 9807, remains.

On its arrival at Galesburg, Illinois, at 7:20 p.m. on November 5, C-ATMCXR0-17 changes crews again, and the DPU is removed for the run to Chicago. From here, the train has just 0.4 horsepower per ton. It departs Galesburg at 9:53 p.m. and arrives back at Cicero at 2:41 a.m. on November 6, almost exactly a week since the empties arrived there from the Norfolk Southern. Since this train has a C-ATMCXR0-17 symbol, its course will vary on the loaded end of the cycle, and from it here it will be interchanged with CSX. In another day it will unload at River Rouge and then begin heading west again.

123

Union Pacific train CBTFG9-03, bound for Oklahoma Gas & Electric at Fort Gibson, Oklahoma, begins loading at Arch Coal's Black Thunder Mine on October 3, 2008. Trains at Black Thunder are loaded by crews provided by Savage Transportation Management, who work closely with mine crews and both BNSF and Union Pacific to keep operations fluid. *Patrick Yough*

(Black Thunder operates the largest working dragline in the United States, a Bucyrus-Erie 2570WS, nicknamed Ursa Major. This unique machine uses a 390-foot boom and 160-cubic-yard bucket to move more than 7,000 cubic yards of overburden an hour.)

The ability of Black Thunder to pump out unit coal trains is impressive. On average, the mine unearths 3 tons of coal a second.

ON AVERAGE, 18 TO 20 UNIT TRAINS DEPART BLACK THUNDER EVERY 24 HOURS, WEIGHING IN THE VICINITY OF 15,000 TONS EACH.

As many as 8 trains are accommodated within the mine trackage at any one time, and 2 individual trains can be loaded simultaneously. The mine may load an entire unit train in just under 75 minutes. An average 18 to 20 unit trains depart Black Thunder every 24 hours. These are typical of those loaded in the Powder River Basin, weighing in the vicinity of 15,000 tons each. As of 2008, Arch Coal estimated that more than 9 million coal hoppers have taken coal from the mine. Arch Coal has expanded by adding the new Black Thunder West load-out, located on the west side of the Joint Line at Reno Junction, which loaded its first train on November 15, 2008.

Even more impressive is the output at NARM. By 2005 this

A Union Pacific unit train passes the new Black Thunder West load-out at Reno Junction, Wyoming. This new load-out filled its first train on November 15, 2008. It was designed with the capability to accommodate five trains awaiting loading. *Patrick Yough*

had exceeded the Black Thunder mine by delivering more than 80 million tons a year. In 2007, it set a world record by delivering 91.5 million tons. This mine taps a coal seam approximately 100 feet thick. BNSF's *Guide to Coal Mines* reports that typical carbon content of this coal is 36.7 percent. Moisture content is 27.4 percent, ash content is 4.4 percent, and sulfur is just 0.2 percent. The mine's twin loading loops can load 2 trains simultaneously, and as many as 12 trains can be queued up for loading within the mine complex. Powder River Coal Company reports that it can load up to 5,900 coal cars daily.

In a morning silhouette on October 1, 2003, BNSF empties wait at Rozet, Wyoming, to return to the Powder River mines for reloading. In 2007, Wyoming's 20 coal mines produced nearly 453.6 million tons of coal, making it the most productive coal state in the country and more productive than the entire Appalachia coal region. *Howard Ande*

An eastbound loaded train arrives at Union Pacific's Bailey Yard in North Platte, Nebraska. Bailey is the largest classification yard in the world, with an average of 155 trains passing through daily, including 70 coal trains. Long-distance coal trains from the Powder River and Uintah basins receive Federal Railroad Administration–required 1,500-mile train inspections here. *Michael L. Gardner*

PRB Unit Trains

Enormous open mines in the PRB and high-volume electric-generating stations are especially conducive to unit train operation. BN's PRB era began with a unit coal train operation from the Belle Ayr Mine to the Comanche Generating Station at Minnequa, Colorado, near Pueblo, a facility operated by the Public Service of Colorado.

In the early days of BN's PRB coal operations, a typical unit coal train consisted of 105 cars. During the mid-1980s, this was gradually increased so that by the early 1990s coal trains were regularly running up to 117 cars. Today, 135-car unit trains are standard.

Longer trains offer increased capacity and economies of scale. Why not just run really long trains then? This is not as simple as it seems. Lengthening standard train length puts strains on equipment and infrastructure, this requires investment and innovation that can take years to implement. Increasing coal train consists from 105 to 135 cars was made possible by several evolutionary changes, including the development of substantially more powerful locomotives. The consulting company Canac (formerly a subsidiary of

Above: December 15, 1993, finds loaded Burlington Northern unit train symbol RR140 behind C30-7 No. 5015 at milepost 238 on former Colorado & Southern trackage east of Barela, Colorado. It is destined for the West Texas Utilities generating station at Oklaunion, Texas, 40 miles west of Wichita Falls. BN's Twin Mountain Subdivision is a key part of a north–south route for Powder River coal traveling to Texas. *John Leopard*

Below: Houston Lighting & Power Company's massive generating station at Smithers Lake, Texas, was one of BN's best Powder River coal customers in that state. Prior to the BNSF merger, BN turned the train over to the Santa Fe at Fort Worth for delivery. HL&P trains used ACF Coalveyor bathtub hoppers owned by the railroad's Utility Fuels subsidiary and identified with UFIX reporting marks. In the background is Colorado's Comanche plant (operated by the Public Service Company of Colorado, now Xcel Energy). *John Leopard*

BN SD70MAC No. 9558 glides westward over a small lake east of Crystal Springs, North Dakota, on May 21, 1999. The train, symbol E-BENBSM0-31, unloaded at the Northern States Power Sherburne County plant at Becker, Minnesota, and is returning empty to Big Sky Mine to reload its 115 coal cars. *Chris Guss*

Canadian National and now owned by Savage Transportation Management) was commissioned to make studies to address the constraints of physical plant and project growth. For example, yard tracks and passing siding were lengthened to enable operation of longer trains. It's one thing to assemble a 135-car train, but it's another to find places where two 135-car trains can pass one another on a single-track main line when sidings have been based on 105-car train lengths. In addition, the mines made substantial investment by building additional holding tracks to speed the loading process. In a related change, many of the larger mines began to utilize contract operators to provide crews for loading.

Since coal is shipped to a multitude of destinations, it is quite normal for loaded PRB coal trains to pass one another on the Orin Cutoff. On face value this

Kansas City Southern Nos. 736 and 722 lead a loaded coal train at Antioch, Nebraska, on August 13, 1992, destined for the Southwestern Electric Power Company plant at Welsh, Texas. Since KCS serves a number of electricity-generating stations, its has been common to find KCS locomotives running through on Burlington Northern and BNSF unit coal trains for more than two decades. Antioch is located in the Nebraska Sand Hills region, which covers more than 20,000 square miles, making it the most extensive sand dunes in the Western Hemisphere. *John Leopard*

might seem strange, but keep in mind that not all coal is of equal value. There are 17 coal mines in the PRB, in addition to mines located along BNSF on lines north of the Orin Cutoff. Coal can differ greatly from mine to mine depending on carbon value, impurities, and sulfur, water, and ash content. Coal suitable to burn in one plant might not be suitable for another. These considerations, along with pricing, help determine the destination, and thus routing, for specific trains.

BNSF's Alliance Hub

Burlington Northern developed its Alliance (Nebraska) Terminal as a primary hub for unit coal train operations. This former CB&Q regional hub serves lines radiating in three directions, all of which were developed as important coal corridors.

Today, Alliance is a railroad oasis in western Nebraska and a major BNSF staging area for Powder River Basin coal operations. Roughly 15 percent of the town's population is employed directly by BNSF, and there are approximately 600 locomotive engineers and conductors based here. BNSF has train-crew pools for runs in all three directions. Southward crews run 128 miles to Guernsey, Wyoming, or 114 miles to Sterling, Colorado. Eastward, crews run 238 miles to Ravenna, Nebraska, and westward they run 111 miles to Edgemont, South Dakota, over Crawford Hill. Here, the 1.55 percent ruling grade eastbound slows

At Northport, Nebraska, a car man makes repairs to a Buckeye coupler on a Midwest Generation empty unit train during the FRA-mandated 1,500-mile train inspection. *Patrick Yough*

used for holding unit trains and primarily serves to stage movements on the Alliance–Northport route, including loaded trains heading south and loaded trains arriving from the south, and to adjust empty unit train consists to their ideal length. Since unit train lengths vary, it is common to adjust train lengths before they return to the mine for reloading. A typical unit set may be adjusted by between 1 to 10 cars. The North Yard is primarily used to stage loaded coal trains headed eastward toward Ravenna.

How much traffic passes through Alliance? Take February 13, 2005, when 67 trains departed this terminal. Of these trains, 26 went east toward Ravenna, 21 were loaded unit coal trains carrying from 110 to 135 cars, and 24 trains headed west toward Edgemont (all except 4 of these were empty unit trains heading back toward the PRB for reloading). Another 17 empty unit trains headed south toward Northport, also for loading at PRB mines.

Modern Diesels Move Coal

In the 1970s and early 1980s, Burlington Northern bought hundreds of new Electro-Motive Division SD40-2s and General Electric U30C and C30-7s for general service and for PRB coal work. Most BN coal trains were hauled by quintets of these cookie-cutter 3,000-horsepower, six-motor, DC-traction diesels. In the first decade of BN's PRB coal operations, these diesels, dressed in the railroad's standard Cascade green-and-white livery, seemed as common as the coal they moved. In the late 1980s, BN augmented its coal fleet with Electro-Motive SD60s leased from Oakway and painted in an attractive blue-and-white scheme similar to the contemporary Electro-Motive demonstrator livery. In the early 1990s, these were joined by a fleet of state-of-the-art SD60Ms equipped with modern safety cabs. Originally, the SD60Ms were based at Glendive, Montana, and largely assigned to coal trains traversing the Northern Pacific route. Now, nearly two decades later, some of these locomotives are routinely assigned as Crawford Hill helpers.

heavy coal trains to a crawl, requiring manned helpers to assist at the back of unit trains. Helper crews are based at Crawford.

Depending on their point of origin, loaded unit coal trains may enter Alliance via one of two routes. Those coming off the north end of the Orin Cutoff or from points west of Donkey Creek Junction are typically routed via Edgemont over Crawford Hill, while those off the south end of the Orin Cutoff heading toward Lincoln run via Wendover and Northport.

The modern Alliance Yard features two primary operational facilities: the South Yard follows the alignment of the Alliance–Northport line, while the North Yard is on the east–west Lincoln–Crawford–Gillette route. The South Yard consists of 20 tracks

In June 1996, a Union Pacific Dash 8-40C leads a mix of Oakway SD60s and Burlington Northern SD40-2s on a loaded BNSF coal train ascending Crawford Hill, Nebraska. Interchanged from Union Pacific at Northport, Nebraska, this train cycle runs from Kansas Power and Light's Jeffery, Kansas, facility on the Union Pacific and Eagle Butte Mine on BNSF. *Scott R. Snell*

Chicago & North Western also assigned SD40-2s and, in the mid-1980s ordered fleets of more modern and nominally more powerful 3,800-horsepower Electro-Motive SD60s. In the late-1980s, C&NW tried something different and began ordering large numbers of GE's modern microprocessor-controlled six-motor-type locomotives, beginning with the Dash 8-40C. C&NW's close relationship with Union Pacific found UP's six-motor units often working through to the PRB in coal service, and at times in the 1980s and 1990s it was nearly as common to find UP units on C&NW coal trains as C&NW's own locomotives.

The great weight of PRB unit trains, combined with the growing number of trains and the large, graded territory they traversed, led BN to investigate more efficient ways of moving trains. Traditionally,

North American diesel-electrics had always used direct-current (DC) traction systems. The Electro-Motive SD40-2s and SD60s, as well as various GE models, all used standard DC-traction systems. As the result of developments in Europe and increasing demands for power and greater efficiency, BN urged Electro-Motive to push the envelope of modern diesel-electric design and adapt three-phase alternating-current (AC) traction systems for North American heavy applications.

131

On May 19, 1990—five years before the BNSF merger—a mix of Burlington Northern GE and Electro-Motive six-motor diesels works northward on Santa Fe's Galveston Subdivision, approaching the former Missouri-Kansas-Texas crossing at Sealy, Texas. This train just met a southbound Santa Fe manifest and is easing out of the siding. Earlier in the day, it delivered coal to Houston Lighting & Power's W. A. Parish plant at Smithers Lake southeast of Rosenberg, Texas, and is returning to the Wyoming coalfields. *Tom Kline*

For many years DC traction had been preferred because of its lower initial cost and relative ease of motor control. Locomotive designers, however, had long been aware of the inherent advantages offered by AC motors. Not only are they simpler than comparable DC motors, but they require less maintenance and tend to be more durable. AC motors also offer greater potential output than DC motors of the same size. But one of the most important characteristics of AC motors for railroad traction applications is their inherent ability to automatically correct for locomotive wheel slip, thereby allowing for much greater adhesion. This characteristic allows an AC-traction locomotive much greater tractive effort than a comparable DC locomotive. Greater pulling power and high tractive effort are especially desirable for very heavy trains on steeply graded lines. Modern developments in control technology finally allowed another look at three-phase AC motors for heavy-haul American locomotives.

In the 1970s, German research in three-phase AC traction resulted in significant technological advances made possible by melding new thyristor and microprocessor technologies to create improved motor control systems. These developments were initially focused on development of electric locomotives where conventional single-phase AC was drawn from catenary (overhead electric wires), converted to DC power, and then inverted to a form of polyphase AC power. Motor speed was controlled by modulating AC current frequency.

General Motors' Electro-Motive Division had experimented with three-phase AC motors in the mid-1970s. Significantly, during the late 1980s and early 1990s, it built AC prototypes using a variation on the traction system developed by the German electric firm Siemens AG. Among these were four SD60MACs, painted for Burlington Northern and tested in PRB coal service. Impressed, BN provided EMD with the necessary financial commitment to

Above: On June 12, 2008, the conductor of an empty coal train inspects a loaded BNSF unit train led by brand-new SD70ACe diesels climbing east on Montana Rail Link's Winston Hill at Winston, Montana. In 1987, Burlington Northern spun off much of its former Northern Pacific main line between Billings, Montana, and Sand Point, Idaho, to regional startup MRL, yet the company retained an operating arrangement allowing its through traffic to continue to use the route. In recent years this has blossomed as a corridor for Powder River coal, with BNSF utilizing the agreement to minimize congestion on parallel routes. *Tom Kline*

Left: A BNSF unit train snakes its way through the Badlands at Sully Springs, North Dakota, on May 20, 1999. Shoving hard on the rear is BN SD40-2 No. 7193, which was cut in at Glendive, Montana. Helpers are used on some eastward coal loads on the 1.11 percent Beaver Hill and 1.06 percent Fryberg Hill grades on the Dickinson Subdivision. By 2008, DPUs in this corridor had reduced but not eliminated the need for manned helpers. *Chris Guss*

further refine a practical AC-traction diesel-electric. While locomotive manufacturers have occasionally pursued new technologies that offered great promise only to find they fall short on application, Electro-Motive's new SD70MAC quickly proved to be a dramatic step forward.

Superior adhesion afforded by the 4,000-horsepower SD70MACs allowed three of this model to effectively perform the same work as five 3,000-horsepower 1970s-era Electro-Motive SD40-2s or

Aluminum Hoppers

The first aluminum hopper car was built in 1934 by the Baltimore & Ohio at the Mt. Clare Shops in Baltimore, in conjunction with Alcoa. Both the body and the underframe were constructed of aluminum alloys (modern aluminum hoppers and rotary gondola cars used today are constructed with a carbon-steel center sill). Although B&O's aluminum experiment was 7 tons lighter than the all-steel version of the same car, it was not repeated and remained a curious anomaly. It was nearly another 35 years before aluminum cars were built to haul coal. In 1985, Bethlehem Steel designed an aluminum variation of its popular steel BethGon coal car. Production began in 1986, with the first cars built for Jacksonville Electric Authority.

As demand for coal from the Powder River Basin increased, the western railroads needed money to expand their physical plants, so they gave the utilities incentives in the form of decreased rates to own their own cars. By converting to the new aluminum cars, the railroads realized a fuel savings, since the new aluminum BethGon's had almost a 33 percent savings in tare weight over the all-steel design.

The railroads were also upgrading their track structure to accommodate 286,000-pound gross rail loading (GRL). This precipitated a new round of car-building to convert original Powder River Basin steel-car fleets to aluminum cars. By 2008, more than 90 percent of the steel fleet on

The dirtiest jobs in a coal-fired power plant are in the coal-handling department, where coal handlers unload hopper cars and distribute coal on the stockpile. They must remain alert to prevent fires while moving coal into the bunkers for storage. NRG Energy honored its coal handlers by naming railcars in recognition of their important contributions to the company. Employees with more than 10 years of service have their name applied to four company hoppers and are given a model of the car. *Patrick Yough*

western coal lines had been phased out in favor of aluminum-body cars. Steel rotary gondolas formerly in PRB service have been reassigned to other services and are often used to haul scrap metal or construction debris.

In 2008, coal-hauling fleets have a roughly even balance between rotary gondolas and bottom-discharge hoppers. In recent years, eastern utilities converting to Powder River coal have largely favored the acquisition of Rapid Discharge bottom-dump cars, in part because when they burned Appalachian coal, they traditionally used railroad-supplied three-bay steel hoppers.

On November 21, 1993, BN C30-7 No. 5528, along with two SD40-2s, leads train 50TT284 at Neilson, Illinois. The coal is bound for Public Service of Indiana from Black Thunder Mine. Southern Illinois coalfields are a shadow of what they used to be, and unit trains like this now pass through the region rather than originating here. *Mike Abalos*

GE U30C/C30-7s. Published statistics indicate that an SD40-2 produces 87,150 pounds of continuous tractive effort; by comparison, an SD70MAC can develop up to 137,000 pounds of tractive effort, thanks to greater adhesion afforded through superior motor control and advanced wheel-slip systems. More significant, however, is that the operating characteristics of its AC motors mean that an SD70MAC will not suffer from limitations imposed by short-time motor ratings. This allows an SD70MAC to maintain very high tractive effort indefinitely and operate at maximum throttle at slow speeds without time penalty.

In addition to greater tractive effort, AC-traction motors offer other important advantages over conventional DC traction, including much more effective dynamic braking at slow speed and longer motor service life. These advantages reduce operational costs and potentially save money. But those potential savings come at a higher per-unit price—a new SD70MAC costs significantly more than a comparable Electro-Motive DC-traction locomotive. For this reason, BN limited application of its AC-traction SD70MACs to heavy unit train services where it could make the most of its investment.

Initially, BN ordered 350 SD70MACs, and the first machines were delivered in December 1993. Their success led BN and its successor, Burlington Northern Santa Fe, to place significant repeat orders.

Chicago & North Western took a different approach. It had garnered good results from GE's Dash 8-40C and in 1993 placed significant orders for GE's latest DC-traction model, the Dash 9-40CW. Railroad observers were impressed because these were the first "safety cab" locomotives ordered by C&NW. Initially these modern machines were assigned to PRB service and could be seen lined up at C&NW's PRB hub at Bill, Wyoming, waiting to bring loaded trains east.

GE's Dash 8 line had introduced microprocessor control to optimize locomotive performance by obtaining information from a variety of sources and providing calculated control of engine speed, cooling functions, and wheel slip, thus offering a degree of precision not available through traditional means. By 1993, GE had introduced several design options and improvements to its Dash 8 design and decided to apply these refinements the new Dash 9 line.

C&NW was one of the first customers to buy GE's basic six-axle, 4,400-horsepower offering. The Dash 9 featured a new high-adhesion truck, split cooling, electronic fuel injection, and an improved step design to make it easier to board the locomotive. The success of its Dash 9s led C&NW to make a final acquisition of 30 AC4400CWs, GE's first commercial AC-traction model. These arrived on the property only a few months before C&NW was officially absorbed into the Union Pacific system in spring 1995.

Where C&NW had assigned its Dash 9s to coal service, UP was quick to blend these locomotives into its road pool. Also, UP, like BN, was keen to take advantage of AC traction in coal service and by the mid-1990s was ordering large numbers of both GE and Electro-Motive AC-traction models, many of which went to work in the PRB.

Following the widespread application of SD70MACs in coal service in the mid-1990s, BNSF reassigned older BN SD60Ms to Crawford Hill helper service, typically in sets of three coupled with a fuel tender. BN's later SD60Ms, identified by a two-piece windshield, have worked in road pool and transcon services. *Michael L. Gardner*

Crawford Hill Helpers

Many people envision Nebraska as a pool-table-level plain. Certainly this is true of much of the state, but western Nebraska has some notable hills. While these are mere pimples compared to the Rocky Mountains, they present operational difficulties for BNSF. Helper locomotives are based at Crawford to assist loaded trains. Typically, these shove at the back. In the early years of Burlington Northern's PRB unit train operations, helpers were typically sets of three SD40-2s. These standard models were reliable, powerful, well-suited to the rigors of graded operation. For the 14-mile shove, these locomotives would be in "run 8" (maximum throttle) and roaring at the back of 110 loaded cars. For a few years in the late 1980s and early 1990s, BN experimented with its helper power. Among the trials

were tank cars equipped as large-capacity fuel tenders that ran mid-consist to minimize refueling stops.

In 1994 and 1995, with the new SD70MACs coming on line in large numbers, BN replaced the SD40-2s with pairs of SD70MACs. Two SD70MACs produce 8,000 horsepower, but since they deliver exceptional tractive effort, they are well-suited for relatively slow-speed, high-adhesion helper applications. During inclement weather when rain or snow coats the rails, SD70MAC helpers have had to make the most of their high-adhesion abilities where wheel-slip control systems make thousands of small motor-output corrections a minute to maintain traction. In more recent times, BNSF has assigned a variety of modern six-motor road locomotives as Crawford Hill helpers, including its SD60Ms and various GE models. Since many unit trains now run with two modern six-motor diesels on the head end and a single unit as a distributed power unit (DPU) at the back, it is common on Crawford Hill to see four units at the back of loaded trains, three of which are the manned helpers.

On September 28, 2008, Montana Rail Link SD70ACe No. 4300 leads the second part of a westward BNSF coal train ascending Mullan Pass at Fort Harrison, Montana. In 2008, operations on Mullan Pass typically saw heavy trains separated into two parts and helpers cut in to shove over the pass. While the first half uses BNSF locomotives, the second half uses MRL locomotives to lead. *Mark Leppert*

Union Pacific SD40-2s Nos. 3376 and 3372, working east with coal loads, pass an empty train at Cozad, Nebraska, on July 19, 1985. *C. Richard Neumiller*

Distributed Power in the PRB

Significant for modern PRB operations is the widespread application of distributed power unit technology—radio-controlled remote helpers operated with GE-Harris Locotrol III technology. Using Locotrol, the locomotive engineer at the head end can operate remote helpers in the middle or back of the train. Not only have DPUs minimized the need for manned helpers, they have assisted in overcoming traditional drawbar limitations, thus enabling BNSF and UP to run much longer, heavier unit trains. DPUs also offer braking advantages. Although there have been great advances in dynamic braking—where

On July 1, 2005, BNSF train C-BTMCNM0-64, which originated at Black Thunder Mine in the Powder River Basin, grinds upgrade east of Red Oak, Iowa. It is heading east to Chicago where it will be interchanged to Norfolk Southern for delivery to Detroit Edison's power plant at River Rouge, Dearborn, Michigan. The two ES44DCs leading the train are DC-traction diesels temporarily assigned to coal duties during 2005 to make up for the lack of AC-traction units normally assigned to BNSF's coal pool. *Chris Guss*

locomotive motors are used as generators to slow a train—North American railroads still stop trains using modern adaptations of the Westinghouse automatic air brake. Significantly, DPUs positioned at both ends of the train aid in braking by setting air brakes more quickly because air enters the train line simultaneously from both ends. This allows long coal trains with DPUs to stop safely more quickly. On the down side, some engineers indicate there have appeared to be more instances of unintended emergency air-brake applications that bring a loaded train to complete and unscheduled stops.

Two sets of DPUs can be seen on a loaded 115-car Union Pacific coal train negotiating the Joint Line at milepost 49 near Palmer Lake, Colorado, on September 18, 2008. This route melds former Santa Fe and Rio Grande lines, and at several locations, tracks follow separate alignments. In this view the rear DPUs are on former Santa Fe right-of-way, while mid-train DPUs are aligned on former D&RGW right-of-way. *Philip A. Brahms*

Dakota, Minnesota & Eastern Eyes the PRB

Although access to the Powder River Basin has been the exclusive domain of BN/BNSF and C&NW/UP, a potential new player for coal traffic made headlines in the 1990s and early twenty-first century. The Dakota, Minnesota & Eastern was one of several regional railroads that emerged in the 1980s as a result of Class 1 spinoffs following passage of the Staggers Act. In 1986, C&NW sold hundreds of miles of lightly used lines across Minnesota and South Dakota to the newly created DM&E. Ten years later, DM&E acquired additional former C&NW trackage in South Dakota and Wyoming from Union Pacific. Although its primary traffic has been grain and agricultural products, in 1997, DM&E shocked the industry with a proposal to reach the Powder River Basin by constructing 280 miles of new trackage and upgrading 600–650 miles of its existing lines. Such construction is subject to regulatory approval, and DM&E filed its detailed plan with the Surface Transportation Board (STB) in 1998. Although STB initially approved the proposal in 2002, the decision was reversed by court actions. In the meantime, DM&E had expanded its system with the acquisition of former Milwaukee Road lines from Kansas City to Chicago and the Twin Cities operated as a subsidiary called Iowa, Chicago

& Eastern. (Canadian Pacific had shed these lines in the mid-1990s, but the regional railroad that operated them for a few years had floundered.)

Finally, in January 2007, a U.S. Appeals Court upheld the approval of DM&E's plan, but a few months later DM&E suffered a significant setback when the Federal Railroad Administration denied the railroad's request for more than $2 billion on the grounds that DM&E's scheme posed an unacceptably high risk for taxpayers.

The vision of a third player in the PRB took on a new dimension in September 2007 when Canadian Pacific announced that it planned to acquire DM&E and its subsidiaries. CP's president and chief executive officer, Fred Green, left little doubt as to the reason for CP's intended acquisition, saying, "Canadian Pacific is excited about the prospect for growth in the coal rich Powder River Basin." On October 30, 2008, Canadian Pacific took operational control of the DM&E.

Chapter 6
UINTAH BASIN COAL

The Uintah Basin is located in eastern Utah and western Colorado, south of the Uintah Range (unique as the only North American mountain range that runs from east to west instead of north to south). Coal found in this region is low in sulfur, ash, and moisture content, has a heating value greater than Powder River Basin coal, and has been used for both electrical generation and metallurgical applications.

Back in 1871, when William Jackson Palmer was pushing his infant Denver & Rio Grande narrow gauge southward from Denver, coal reserves were known to exist in the region. Although mining traffic dominated the mindset of Colorado railroad builders in the late nineteenth century, it was mostly silver, not coal, that encouraged D&RG and other lines over the high passes of the Rockies.

Palmer had visions of a direct line from Denver to Mexico and hoped to establish a 3-foot gauge empire across the American Southwest, with branches to tap mineral wealth in the mountains, while building a westward connection with the Central Pacific to reach the Pacific Ocean. Regular service on the D&RG to Colorado Springs began on January 1, 1872. Later that year, the tracks reached Pueblo, 118 miles south of Denver, and a branch was constructed

Utah Railway No. 9005 catches the last rays of sunlight at a mine load-out near Castle Gate, Utah. In the business of moving coal since 1914, Utah Railway expanded its operations in 1996 as a result of new trackage rights gained through the Union Pacific–Southern Pacific merger. *Scott R. Snell*

from Pueblo toward Canyon City to tap nearby mines both for locomotive fuel and as a source of potential traffic for the fledgling railway. Additional coal deposits in the Trinidad Field had been identified as a source of coking coal.

In its early years D&RG vied with Santa Fe for territory. The competition dashed Palmer's dreams of a through line to Mexico, so instead he built west, reaching Salt Lake City in 1883. Denver & Rio Grande reached peak narrow gauge mileage in 1889 when it briefly operated 1,861 miles of 3-foot gauge trackage (including dual gauge sections). Although useful for reaching remote mountain mining communities, 3-foot gauge proved inadequate for moving through traffic. By 1890, roughly 600 miles of D&RG narrow gauge had been converted to standard gauge. In places, Rio Grande built all-new alignments to give it a suitable standard gauge main line from Denver to Salt Lake City by way of Pueblo, the Royal Gorge, and Tennessee Pass, although some narrow gauge lines survived as part of the Rio Grande network until the late 1960s.

After World War I, the railroad was reorganized as the Denver & Rio Grande Western. By this time it had tapped coal mines southeast of Provo, Utah, along its main line over Soldier Summit. Among Rio Grande's customers were blast furnaces at Provo (constructed in 1924) that were routinely supplied with coking coal from Utah mines.

Early in the twentieth century, Denver entrepreneur David Moffat, who entertained visions of building a direct route over the Rockies to Salt Lake,

Above: In September 1996, four new Southern Pacific AC4400CWs work as mid-train DPUs on a loaded unit train ascending Tennessee Pass east of Pando, Colorado. High-altitude operation on a prolonged 3 percent ruling grade has made Tennessee Pass one of the most difficult places in the country to run unit trains. Union Pacific discontinued regular operations over the route in 1997, choosing to route coal trains via the Moffat Route and detouring merchandise traffic via its Wyoming main line. This coal train operated with three AC4400CWs in the lead, four mid-train, and two more at the back. *Brian Solomon*

Opposite: A loaded Southern Pacific coal train follows the Eagle River on its ascent of the west slope of Colorado's Tennessee Pass near Pando. In its final year, SP assigned new AC4400CWs to coal trains working on its Rocky Mountain crossings. In the mid-1990s, coal traffic boomed on Rio Grande lines, partly as a result of SP's creative marketing strategy that moved taconite west from the Minnesota Iron Range to Utah's Geneva Steel and back-hauled coal east in the same hoppers. The arrangement allowed coal shippers in Utah and Colorado to offer attractive low rates to Midwestern consumers. *Brian Solomon*

financed construction of the Denver, Northwestern & Pacific Railway. This climbed over the spine of the Rockies via a nosebleed crossing of the Continental Divide at Rollins Pass, 11,660 feet above sea level. Moffat exhausted his cash well short of his goal. After his death in 1911, his railroad was reorganized as the Denver & Salt Lake. Despite this promising name, by 1914 D&SL had made it only as far as the Yampa coalfields at Craig, Colorado, where the line stalled. Without the benefit of through traffic, the D&SL subsisted on coal that moved via the treacherous Rollins Pass Crossing until 1928, hauled by compact Mallet compounds. Completion of the publicly financed 6-mile-long Moffat Tunnel negated the need for the Rollins Pass grade and its associated difficulties. Rio Grande bought control of the D&SL in the early 1930s and built the Dotsero Cutoff connecting the two lines via Bond. This gave D&RGW a more direct

On September 5, 1992, Rio Grande No. 5403 leads train EYVLC-05 through the double horseshoe between Crater and Bond on the Craig Branch. Upon arrival in Denver the train will be interchanged to the Burlington Northern, which will deliver it to Public Service Company of Colorado's Valmont power plant near Boulder. *Don Marson*

route west from Denver and an easier crossing of the Rockies for heavy freight. D&RGW merged D&SL into its system in 1947.

In 1962, the Rio Grande built a 13-mile branch off the Craig Branch to the new Energy Mine. Known as the Energy Branch or Energy Spur, this branch hosted loaded unit trains traveling east via the Moffat route to power plants in Denver. Another 3-mile branch was constructed south from a junction at Hayden on the Craig Branch to a generating station.

Colorado Coal

Historically the market for Colorado coal has been very susceptible to national and global changes in the fuel market. In a detailed article appearing in the July 1994 issue of *Trains*, Mark Hemphill highlights fluctuations that have affected the sale and transport of Colorado coal. Coal from this region is especially desirable because of its high BTU rating and its low content of undesirable sulfur, ash, and moisture. On the down side, greater difficulties in mining, combined with higher transport costs, have at various times tempered demand. The rise of the oil economy in the 1940s and 1950s also hurt the market for western coal, but the opening of new mines in the early 1960s improved the picture, and over the next decade and a half, Colorado coal shipped by rail steadily increased.

On November 18, 1978, five Rio Grande SD40T-2s lead a train of loaded Rock Island hoppers toward a meet with a westbound freight at Rollinsville, Colorado, on the Moffat Route. *C. Richard Neumiller*

The embargo of Middle East oil contributed to rising oil costs in the 1970s, which further fueled the Colorado coal boom through the end of the decade. In 1970, using American Association of Railroads data, the *Coal Traffic Annual* reported that in 1969 Rio Grande originated 6,460,396 tons of the 7,990,566 tons of coal it carried. At that time, the average carload was just 85 tons. The *1975 Coal Traffic Annual* reported that in 1974, Rio Grande originated 9,202,545 tons, consisting of 97,779 carloads with an average of 94.1 tons per car. Where all-rail movement of coal in Colorado was nearly 4 million tons in 1970, it had reached nearly 6.4 million in 1974. Coal traffic continued to rise as new mines were opened in the Yampa coal field. In 1978, the Rio Grande built its Axial spur to tap new mines.

The Colorado coal boom cooled in the early 1980s with the dramatic rise of Powder River coal, which cut the demand for Colorado mine products. Lower mining and transport costs gave Wyoming coal an advantage despite being of slightly lower quality than Colorado coal. However, within a few years, Colorado coal's high yield and clean-burning qualities helped it secure a place in the market despite the rising tide of cheap Wyoming coal.

In the July 1994 *Trains*, Hemphill highlights six mines active in the Yampa coal field, although two of these were producing for local generating stations and didn't feed the Southern Pacific, which had joined with the Rio Grande in 1988. Most of the Yampa coal that did move by rail fed generating stations near Denver and Colorado Springs, specifically Public Service of Colorado's Cherokee and Arapahoe plants in Denver, and the Valmont plant near Boulder.

This Denver, Rio Grande & Western unit train delivered coal to one of Colorado Springs' two coal-fired power plants at Drake and Nixon. The train loaded near Craig and was routed via Steamboat Springs and Bond, and eastward through the Moffat Tunnel to Denver, reaching its destination on the D&RGW/Santa Fe Joint Line. After unloading, the train returned empty to the mine via the same route. This view at Statebridge on May 31, 1989, shows mid-train helpers on train No. 710 with 100 loads weighing 12,298 tons. On the head end are two SD40T-2s and an SD50. *George S. Pitarys*

Southern Pacific 1EYCKC-10 loads at the Energy Mine on August 10, 1992. This was the first instance where four freshly painted SP locomotives wearing the new "speed lettering" were assigned to coal-train service. The photographer, working as SP's director of locomotive management, organized this special consist for the marketing department. After loading, it ran to Public Service Company of Colorado's Cherokee power plant in Denver. *Don Marson*

Union Pacific Operations

In 1996, Union Pacific bought Southern Pacific and merged their operations. Union Pacific made significant changes to operations on the old Rio Grande. Where SP had routed coal trains and other traffic over the Moffat route and Tennessee Pass, Union Pacific decided to close the Tennessee Pass in 1997 and reroute all eastward coal over the Moffat route, while sending carload and intermodal traffic via its Wyoming main line. UP also discontinued usage of the former Missouri Pacific route east of Pueblo—known in SP times as the Hoisington Subdivision—and upgraded its Kansas Pacific line east of Denver for use as a coal corridor.

Despite some concerns regarding UP's commitment to Colorado and Utah coal, the commodity has continued to ship from Rocky Mountain mines at respectable rates. In 1997, the first full year of the

Southern Pacific 274 west moves empty coal hoppers west of Texas Creek, Colorado, in January 1996. Although an operational headache, Tennessee Pass allowed the Rio Grande (and later the Southern Pacific) direct access to the Pueblo gateway for coal traffic moving to eastern and southern markets. The high operating costs didn't suit Union Pacific, and today Tennessee Pass stands silent. UP routes all eastbound Colorado and Utah coal traffic via the Moffat Tunnel to Denver. *Chris Guss*

UP-SP merger, UP operated a daily average of 10 loaded trains generated on former Rio Grande lines. A decade later, 11 to 15 trains might be found moving on the old Rio Grande on any given day, depending on the season and demand for coal.

In recent years the two most significant Yampa mines supplying UP coal trains on the former Rio Grande Craig Branch have been Colowyo Mine at the end of the Axial Spur and Twentymile Mine on the Energy Spur. Colowyo Mine is a surface

Union Pacific's former Rio Grande Moffat Tunnel route has developed as an intensely traveled coal funnel. Every day, 20 to 24 trains—mostly unit trains loaded at Colorado and Utah mines—transit this busy mountain crossing. Here, a pair of Union Pacific GEs leads a coal train at Moffat's east portal in June 2000. *Michael L. Gardner*

operation that produced 4.5 million tons in 1995, the last full year of SP operations of the Rio Grande. In 2008, Union Pacific reported this mine has capacity for 9 million tons annually. Trains are loaded using a single-track loading loop designed for 110-car trains that are loaded at a rate of up to 7,000 tons per hour.

Twentymile Mine is located at Oak Creek and loads trains at Energy, Colorado. Part of the Twentymile complex is the

UNION PACIFIC TRAINS AT TWENTYMILE MINE ARE LOADED AT A RATE OF UP TO 7,000 TONS PER HOUR.

Foidel Creek Mine, which opened for production in 1983 and was substantially improved in 1996. Union Pacific lists Twentymile annual production as 8.5 to 9 million tons and cites annual production in 2001 of 7.5 million tons.

In 2007, Union Pacific figures indicated that the railroad operated an average of 80 loaded trains per month on the Craig Branch. In October 2008, UP operated 87 trains, compared with an abnormally low figure of 60 trains in September.

In recent years, significant elements of Union Pacific's Colorado coal operations have been mines in the western part of the state, especially along its North Fork Branch, which runs southeasterly from Grand Junction. These mines include Bowie No. 2

On February 24, 1996, the massive Commonwealth Edison Kincaid generating station provides a backdrop for Chicago & Illinois Midland Nos. 30 and 53 as they back cars into the coal-unloading equipment at C&IM's Ellis Yard. The coal originated on Southern Pacific in Utah and was interchanged to C&IM at Ridgely Tower in Springfield, Illinois. This was at a time when SP was moving Utah coal as a backhaul for Minnesota iron ore moving to Utah's Geneva Steel. Electricity from this plant is consumed in Chicago, more than 100 miles away. *Scott Muskopf*

Union Pacific convertible SD9043AC operates as a DPU on train CPAWE9-25, an empty on the former Rio Grande Moffat Route at Coal Creek, Colorado, west of Denver. It's en route from Paducah, Kentucky, to Arch Coal's West Elk Mine at Arco, Colorado. *Patrick Yough*

Mine, Elk Creek Mine, and West Elk Mine. Bowie No. 2 Mine was opened for production in November 1997. According to UP in 2008, its production capacity is 6 million tons per year. Trains are loaded on a single-ended siding at the Converse load-out. Typically, Bowie trains run at a maximum of 105 cars.

Situated near Somerset, Colorado, Elk Creek Mine opened in 2003 and is one of the newest large mines on the former Rio Grande in Colorado. As of 2008, this underground mine produced about 6 million tons annually and loaded 115-car unit trains.

The West Elk Mine is an underground mine that opened in 1982. UP reported that it has production capacity of 7 million tons, and in 2001 it produced just over 5 million tons. It can load up to 5,500 tons per hour and like the Bowie Mine is served by 105-car unit trains. In 2008, the North Fork mines produced more coal for Colorado than the Craig Branch. By October, 114 unit trains were loaded each month on average.

Utah Coal

Contemporary mines in central Utah produce some of the largest volume of traffic along former Rio Grande lines. Union Pacific loaded 151 trains in Utah during July 2008. Although this was a high figure—130 trains per month was more typical—it demonstrates the importance of Utah coal on the old Rio Grande, where unit coal trains have been the dominant freight since the late 1990s when UP shifted through merchandise and intermodal traffic to its Wyoming main line.

Union Pacific serves Dugout Canyon Mine near Price. Using conveyors, the underground mine serves rail-loading points at the Banning load-out and Savage Coal Terminal. The latter facility has a loading loop that can accommodate unit trains up to 110 cars. Annual mine production capacity is estimated at 1.25 million tons. Horizon Mine began production in 1998 and loads at the CV Spur. Annual production capacity is about 1 million tons, and it loads unit trains up to 105 cars.

In April 1995, Belt Railway of Chicago Alco C-424s deliver Southern Pacific coal to the KCBX terminal at South Chicago. This was part of a complex circuit operated by SP and Wisconsin Central using hoppers to move coal east and taconite from the Minnesota Iron Range west to Utah's Geneva Steel. *John Leopard*

Among the larger Utah mines is Skyline Mine near Scofield, which produces up to 5.5 million tons annually. Sufco Mine is in Sevier County and loads trains at Sharp, near Levan, Utah. This mine complex has been active since 1941 and can produce up to 6.5 million tons annually. The mine loads unit trains up to 115 cars.

Utah Railway

In 1912, the Utah Railway was organized to build into the coalfields in Utah's Carbon and Emery counties and provide a connection for the San Pedro, Los Angeles & Salt Lake—essentially part of the Union Pacific system. Although it originally planned to build its own line over Soldier Summit, instead Utah Railway and Rio Grande worked out a deal that improved the existing route over the pass and expanded capacity using double-track. This gave Utah Railway a mix of joint access and trackage rights between Utah Railway Junction (near Helper) and Provo. Utah Railway's own coal-hauling lines were largely complete by 1914.

Utah Railway has been a consistent mover of coal in the region. As a result of the UP-SP merger, in

On September 30, 1995, Utah Railway F45 No. 9013 leads empties between Kyune and Lynn on Subdivision 6 over Soldier Summit. These were received from Union Pacific at Provo. The train operated east to Utah Railway Junction, where it continued on Utah Railway's line to the Wildcat load-out for reloading. *Don Marson*

1996 the Utah Railway gained more extensive trackage rights, allowing it to operate as far east as Grand Junction, Colorado, and access to greater numbers of mines, including the Dugout Mine's Savage load-out. In 2002, the railroad was bought by Genesee & Wyoming, a short-line operating company. Today, the railroad can interchange coal trains at both Provo and Grand Junction, and it connects with BNSF. It routinely operates at least one daily unit train that can run up to 105 cars. Its westward trains over Soldier Summit typical run with a four-unit mid-train helper.

Since dieselization, Utah Railway's consistently eclectic motive power has garnered the small coal-hauler an unusual amount of attention from photographers.

Four Utah Railway RSD4s with hoppers are in the yard at Hiawatha, Utah, on July 17, 1978. Although a relatively small player in the movement of Uintah Basin coal, Utah Railway's eclectic diesels have long made it popular with photographers. It was among the last railroads to operate six-motor Alcos, with 244 engines in heavy service. *C. Richard Neumiller*

Eastbound York Canyon coal loads (symbol C-YCCH) pass antique Union Switch & Signal Style T semaphores at Mindeman, Colorado, on December 1, 1993. The train loaded in New Mexico at Pittsburg & Midway Coal Mining Company's York Canyon Mine and was destined for Wisconsin Electric Power Company's station at Oak Creek, Wisconsin, near Milwaukee. The contract to Oak Creek began in September 1992 and saw trains running via Raton Pass, but the service ended in 1996 when coal reserves depleted. *John Leopard*

York Canyon

In 1966 Santa Fe Railway extended a new branch into New Mexico's York Canyon. Known as the York Canyon Sub, the branch ran 36 miles north from a junction at French, New Mexico, with its Las Vegas (New Mexico) Subdivision—part of Santa Fe's original transcontinental route. (Of historical interest, a portion of Santa Fe's York Canyon Sub was laid down on the right-of-way of SP's abandoned line from Tucumcari to Dawson, New Mexico.) Santa Fe's York Canyon Sub served mines noted for very desirable high-yield, low-sulfur coal. In its first couple of decades, York Canyon supplied Santa Fe with unit trains and spot loads for various destinations, including the large Kaiser Steel mill at Fontana, California.

In his *Santa Fe Annual 1992–1993*, Kevin EuDaly details modern York Canyon operations, explaining that in 1991 and 1992, York Canyon mines were expanded in anticipation of increased production to supply Wisconsin Electric Power's Oak Creek power plant. Unit trains to Wisconsin began in September 1992. These consisted of 115 cars and typically required six modern Dash 8s—three on the head end and three as mid-train helpers to negotiate grades on the line. In order to accommodate dimensional constraints imposed by the coal-loading equipment at York Canyon, all of Santa Fe's 800-series Dash 8s featured a specialized cab roofline profile. After loading, trains descended the York Canyon Sub to French, where helpers were needed to aid with dynamic braking.

The most difficult and most dramatic element of the York Canyon move was the ascent of Raton Pass, a rugged line with grades in excess of 3 percent, making it one of the steepest coal lines in the West. To get tonnage over this unusually steep pass, 115-car trains were typically divided at Raton, New Mexico, and doubled over the mountain. Each section had 56 or 57 cars and was brought over the pass using both sets of three Dash 8s. The unit train was reassembled into a full set at Jensen, Colorado, beyond the steepest

One of the most unusual coal operations in the West is Black Mesa & Lake Powell's remote and isolated 78-mile line in the Four Corners area of northern Arizona. On October 12, 1998, an eastbound empty train departs Page, Arizona, behind four GE high-voltage E60C electric locomotives. The railroad was built for the sole purpose of supplying coal to the Navajo generating station near Page. *Howard Ande*

Union Pacific train CCQAI-31 brings empty hoppers from Arizona Electric Power Cooperative's Apache plant to Colorado's Axial Mine. It is pictured during a crew change at Cochise, Arizona (between Tucson and El Paso), on the former Southern Pacific Sunset Route. *Patrick Yough*

grades on the east slope. The combination of short, heavy trains, punishing steep grades, and the latest modern locomotives made for one of the most dramatic operations on the Santa Fe, but it lasted for only a few years. EuDaly indicates that York Canyon trains were intended to supply as much as 3 million tons of coal annually to Wisconsin Electric Power Company for a period of 15 years. However, coal reserves appear to have been overstated, and unit train services concluded several years ahead of plan.

Acknowledgments

A book of this scope could not be researched and assembled without the help of many people. The authors would like to thank everyone who participated for their efforts in making this the best book possible.

Special thanks to Chris Guss for his detail-oriented research and captioning, and for hosting the authors on visits to the Chicago area. Ted Baun of FreightCar America provided details about modern hoppers and rotary gondolas. Sean Robitaille assisted with understanding the complexities of Illinois Basin coal country. Robert Rohauer and Gary Sease provided details and statistics about CSX, as Norfolk Southern's Robin Chapman and Jerry Nassar did for NS. Larry DeYoung provided details of operations on the Western New York & Pennsylvania. Mark Demaline of the Wheeling & Lake Erie helped with his knowledge of southern Ohio coal operations and transfer facilities. T. S. Hoover provided an understanding of operations on old Pennsylvania Railroad, Baltimore & Ohio, Chesapeake & Ohio, Norfolk & Western, and Clinchfield routes. Doug Eisele helped with captioning and details of NORAC Rules, and loaned photos and research materials from his collection. Tim Doherty provided his expertise in coal operations and historical context on the New York, Ontario & Western and Conrail. Tom Mangan provided lodging and navigational skills on a trip to the former Rio Grande. Jonathan Hefti provided details about rotary car dumpers and unloading pits. Thanks to Marshall Beecher for tours of Chicago. Otto Vondrak provided custom-drawn maps. Scott Muskopf provided caption research, with the able assistance of Ryan Crawford, Daniel Kohlberg, John P. Kohlberg, Erik Coleman, and Chuck Grigsby. Special thanks, also, to Kurt Bell, David Dunn, and Nick Zmijewski at the Railroad Museum of Pennsylvania. Steamtown's archivist and historian, Patrick McKnight, helped navigate the extensive Steamtown archive and library. John Gruber made many connections and provided logistical support on Midwestern trips. The Irish Railway Record Society lent use of their Dublin library. Paul Wussow and Bon French assisted with scanning and captioning C. Richard Neumiller's excellent

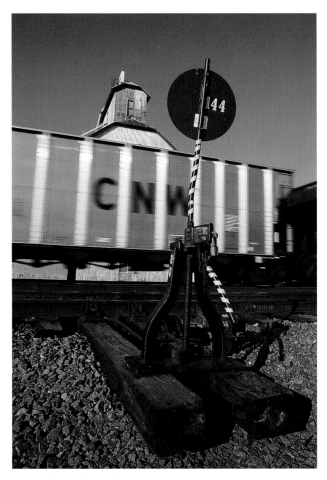

A new Chicago & North Western outside-braced, five-bay, bottom-dump, aluminum hopper blurs past a switch stand in June 1996. *Scott R. Snell*

photographs. Scott Snell not only lent his own material but assisted by hosting slide shows and providing tours of eastern Pennsylvania railroading. Eric Johnson provided insight into barge operations on the Monongahela and upper Ohio rivers. Brian's father, Richard Jay Solomon, has been photographing railways since the 1950s; in addition to providing a wide selection of images for this project, he lent use of his extensive library.

In all, more than 35 photographers lent their work to this project. We pored over more than 5,000 images in an effort to locate the best available illustrations to accompany the text. Each photographer is credited in the captions accompanying their images, and many helped write those captions.

Special thanks go to Pat's parents, James and Betty Yough, for their support and guidance.

Finally, thanks to Dennis Pernu and everyone at Voyageur Press for transforming text and photos into a book!

Bibliography

Books

1846–1896 Fiftieth Anniversary of the Incorporation of the Pennsylvania Railroad Company. Philadelphia: Pennsylvania Railroad, 1896.

Ahrons, E. L. *The British Steam Railway Locomotive 1825–1925.* London: Bracken Books, 1926.

Alexander, Edwin P. *The Pennsylvania Railroad: A Pictorial History, 1st Ed.* New York: W. W. Norton, 1947.

Anderson, Elaine. *The Central Railroad of New Jersey's First 100 Years.* Easton, Pa.: Center for Canal History and Technology, 1984.

Apelt, Brian. *The Corporation: A Centennial Biography of United States Steel Corporation, 1901–2001.* Pittsburgh, Pa., Cathedral Publishing University of Pittsburgh, 2000.

Archer, Robert F. *A History of the Lehigh Valley Railroad: Route of the Black Diamond.* Berkeley, Calif.: Howell-North Books, 1977.

Armstrong, John H. *The Railroad: What It Is, What It Does.* Omaha, Neb.: Simmons-Boardman Publishing, 1982.

Barr, R. E. *Organization and Traffic of the Illinois Central System.* 1938.

Bean, W. L. *Twenty Years of Electrical Operation on the New York, New Haven and Hartford Railroad.* East Pittsburgh, Pa.: Westinghouse Electric & Manufacturing, 1927.

Beaver, Roy C. *The Bessemer & Lake Erie Railroad 1869–1969.* San Marino, Calif.: Golden West Books, 1969.

Beck, John. *Never Before in History: The Story of Scranton.* Northridge, Calif.: Windsor Publications, 1986.

Bednar, Mike. *Anthracite Rebirth: The Story of the Reading and Northern Railroad.* Laurys Station, Pa.: Garrigues House, Publishers, 1998.

Bezilla, Michael. *Electric Traction on the Pennsylvania Railroad 1895–1968.* State College: The Pennsylvania State University Press, 1981.

Bruce, Alfred W. *The Steam Locomotive in America.* New York: Bonanza Books, 1952.

Bryant, Keith L., Jr. *Railroads in the Age of Regulation 1900–1980.* New York: Facts on File, 1988.

Burgess, George, H., and Miles C. Kennedy. *Centennial History of the Pennsylvania Railroad.* Philadelphia: Pennsylvania Railroad, 1949.

Caloroso, Bill. *Pennsylvania Railroad's Elmira Branch.* Andover, N.J.: Andover Junction Publications, 2003.

Casey, Robert J., and W. A. S. Douglas. *The Lackawanna Story.* New York: McGraw-Hill, 1951.

Cassidy, Samuel M. *Elements of Practical Coal Mining.* Baltimore: The American Institute of Mining, Metallurgical, and Petroleum Engineers, 1973.

Castner, Charles B., with Ronald Flanary and Patrick Dorin. *Louisville & Nashville Railroad: The Old Reliable.* Salem, Va.: TLC Publishing, 1996.

A Century of Progress: History of the Delaware and Hudson Company 1823–1923. Albany, N.Y.: Delaware & Hudson, 1925.

Chernow, Ron. *The House of Morgan: An American Banking Dynasty and the Rise of Modern Finance.* New York: Atlantic Monthly Press, 1990.

Churella, Albert, J. *From Steam to Diesel.* Princeton, N.J.: Princeton University Press, 1998.

Clarke, Thomas Curtis, et al. *The American Railway: Its Construction, Development, Management, and Appliances.* New York: Scribner's, 1889.

Cupper, Dan. *Horseshoe Heritage: The Story of a Great Railroad Landmark.* Halifax, Pa.: Withers Publishing, 1996.

Daughen, Joseph R., and Peter Binzen. *The Wreck of the Penn Central.* Boston: Little, Brown, 1971.

Davis, Burke. *The Southern Railway: Road of the Innovators.* Chapel Hill: The University of North Carolina Press,, 1985.

DiCiccio, Carmen. *Coal and Coke in Pennsylvania.* Harrisburg, Pa.: Pennsylvania Historical and Museum Commission, 1996.

Dixon, Thomas W., Jr. *Chesapeake & Ohio: Superpower to Diesels.* Newton, N.J.: Carstens Publications, 1984.

———. *Appalachian Coal Mines & Railroads.* Lynchburg, Va.: TLC Publishing, 1994.

Doherty, Timothy Scott, and Brian Solomon. *Conrail.* St. Paul, Minn.: MBI Publishing Company, 2004.

Dorin, Patrick C., and Robert C. Del Grosso. *Burlington Northern Railroad: Coal Hauler and Coal Country Trackside Guide.* Bonners Ferry, Idaho: Great Northern Pacific Publications, 1995.

Droege, John A. *Freight Terminals and Trains.* New York: McGraw-Hill, 1912.

Drury, George H. *The Historical Guide to North American Railroads.* Waukesha, Wis.: Kalmbach Publishing, 1985.

Ellsworth, Kenneth. *The Car and Locomotive Cyclopedia of American Practices, 4th Ed.* Omaha, Neb. Simmons-Boardman, 1980.

Ermert, Emil R. *The Story of Pioneer Tunnel Coal Mine & Steam Train.* Privately published, 1994 and 2005.

EuDaly, Kevin. *Santa Fe Rails, Vol. 1.* Kansas City, Mo.: White River Productions, 1996.

Farrington, S. Kip., Jr. *Railroading from the Head End.* New York: Doubleday, Doran, 1943.

———. *Railroads at War.* New York: Coward-McCann, 1944.

———. *Railroading from the Rear End.* New York: Coward-McCann, 1946.

———. *Railroads of Today.* New York: Coward-McCann, 1949.

———. *Railroading the Modern Way.* New York: Coward-McCann, 1951.

———. *Railroads of the Hour.* New York: Coward-McCann, 1958.

Ferrell, Mallory Hope. *Colorful East Broad Top.* Forest Park, Ill.: Heimburger House, 1993.

Frey, Robert L. *Railroads in the Nineteenth Century.* New York, 1988.

Grant, H. Roger. *Erie-Lackawanna: Death of an American Railroad.* Stanford, Calif.: Stanford University Press, 1994.

Greenberg, William T., Jr., and Robert F. Fischer. *The Lehigh Valley Railroad East of Mauch Chunk.* Martinsville, N.J.: The Gingerbread Stop, 1997.

Grenard, Ross, and Frederick A. Kramer. *East Broad Top to the Mines and Back.* Newton, N.J.: Carstens Publications, 1990.

Grodinsky, Julius. *Jay Gould: His Business Career 1867–1892.* Philadelphia: University of Pennsylvania Press, 1957.

Hare, Jay V. *History of the Reading.* Philadelphia: John Henry Strock, 1966.

Harlow, Alvin F. *The Road of the Century.* New York: Creative Age Press, 1947.

Helm, Robert A. *The Clinchfield Railroad in the Coal Fields.* Salem, Va.: TLC Publishing, 2004.

Helmer, William F. *O&W: The Long Life and Slow Death of the New York, Ontario and Western Railway, 2nd Ed. Rev.* San Diego: Howell-North, 1959.

Henwood, James N. J. *Laurel Line: An Anthracite Region Railway.* Glendale, Calif.: Interurban Press, 1986.

Hilton, George W. *American Narrow Gauge Railroads.* Stanford, Calif.: Stanford University Press, 1990.

Holton, James L. *The Reading Railroad: History of a Coal Age Empire, Vols. I & II.* Laurys Station, P: Garrigues House, 1992.

Hungerford, Edward. *Daniel Willard Rides the Line.* New York: Putnam, 1938.

———. *Men of Erie: A Story of Human Effort.* New York: Random House, 1946.

Jacobs, Harry A. *The Juniata Canal and Old Portage Railroad.* Hollidaysburg, Pa.: Blair County Historical Society, 1941.

Karig, Martin Robert, III. *Coal Cars: The First Three Hundred Years.* Scranton, Pa.: University of Scranton Press, 2007.

King, Steve. *Clinchfield Country.* Silver Spring, Md.: Old Line Graphics, 1988.

Kilmer, Lawrence W. *Erie Railroad, 1863–1976: Bradford Branch.* Elma, N.Y.: Elma Press, [nd].

Klein, Maury. *History of the Louisville & Nashville Railroad.* New York, 1972.

Kobus, Ken, and Jack Consoli. *The Pennsylvania Railroad's Golden Triangle: Main Line Panorama in the Pittsburgh Area.* Upper Darby, Pa.: The Pennsylvania Railroad Technical and Historical Society, 1998.

Kobus, Ken, and Gary Rauch. *Pennsy's Conemaugh Division.* Upper Darby, Pa.: The Pennsylvania Railroad Technical and Historical Society, 2007.

Lewie, Chris J. *Two Generations on the Allegheny Portage Railroad.* Shippensburg, Pa.: Burd Street Press, 2001.

Loving, Rush, Jr. *The Men Who Loved Trains: The Story of Men Who Battled Greed to Save an Ailing Industry.* Bloomington: Indiana University Press, 2006

Majumdar, Shyamal K., and E. Willard Miller. *Pennsylvania Coal: Resources, Technology, and Utilization.* Easton: Pennsylvania Academy of Science, 1983.

McLean, Harold H. *Pittsburgh & Lake Erie Railroad.* San Marino, Calif.: Golden West Books, 1980.

Mellander, Deane E. *East Broad Top: Slim Gauge Survivor.* Silver Spring, Md.: Old Line Graphics, 1995.

Middleton, William D. *When the Steam Railroads Electrified.* Milwaukee, Wis.: Kalmbach Publishing, 1974.

———. *Landmarks on the Iron Road.* Bloomington: Indiana University Press, 1999.

Middleton, William D., with George M. Smerk and Roberta L. Diehl. *Encyclopedia of North American Railroads.* Bloomington: Indiana University Press, 2007.

Miller, Donald L., and Richard E. Sharpless. *The Kingdom of Coal.* Philadelphia: University of Pennsylvania Press, 1985.

Mohowski, Robert E. *New York, Ontario & Western in the Diesel Age.* Andover, N.J.: Andover Junction Publications, 1994.

Mott, Edward Harold. *Between the Ocean and the Lakes: The Story of Erie.* New York: John S. Collins, 1900.

Overton, Richard, C. *Burlington West.* Cambridge, Mass.: Harvard University Press, 1941.

———. *Burlington Route.* New York: Alfred A. Knopf, 1965.

Pietrak, Paul V. *The History of the Buffalo & Susquehanna Railway.* Privately published, 1966, 1995.

Pietrak, Paul V., with Joseph G. Streamer and James A. Van Brocklin. *Western New York and Pennsylvania Railway.* Privately published, 2000.

Pratt, Edwin A. *American Railways.* London: Macmillan and Company, 1903.

Protheroe, Ernest. *The Railways of the World.* London: Routledge, c. 1914.

Riegel, Robert Edgar. *The Story of the Western Railroads: From 1852 through the Reign of the Giants.* Lincoln: University of Nebraska Press, 1926.

Roberts, Charles S., and Gary W. Schlerf. *Triumph I: Altoona to Pitcairn 1846–1996.* Baltimore: Bernard, Roberts and Company, 1997.

Roberts, Charles S., and David W. Messer. *Triumph VII: 1827–2004—Harrisburg to the Lakes Wilkes-Barre, Oil City and Red Bank.* Baltimore: Bernard, Roberts and Company, 2004.

Rosenberger, Homer Tope. *The Philadelphia and Erie Railroad.* Potomac, Md.: The Fox Hills Press, 1975.

Salisbury, Stephen. *No Way to Run a Railroad: The Untold Story of the Penn Central Crisis.* New York: McGraw-Hill, 1982.

Saunders, Richard, Jr. *The Railroad Mergers and the Coming of Conrail.* Westport, Conn.: Greenwood-Heinemann Publishing, 1978.

———. *Merging Lines: American Railroads 1900–1970.* DeKalb: Northern Illinois University Press, 2001.

Saylor, Roger B. *The Railroads of Pennsylvania.* State College: Pennsylvania State University Press, 1964.

Shaughnessy, Jim. *Delaware & Hudson.* Berkeley, Calif.: Howell-North Books, 1967.

———. *Sylvester Welch's Report on the Allegheny Portage Railroad.* Gettysburg, Pa.: Thomas Publications, 1975.

Sinclair, Angus. *Development of the Locomotive Engine.* Cambridge, Mass.: MIT Press, 1970.

Snell, J. B. *Early Railways.* London: Octopus Publishing, 1972.

Solomon, Brian. *The American Steam Locomotive.* Osceola, Wis.: MBI Publishing Company, 1998.

———. *Railway Masterpieces: Celebrating the World's Greatest Trains, Stations and Feats of Engineering.* Iola, Wis.: Krause Publications, 2002.

———. *Railroad Signaling.* St. Paul, Minn.: MBI Publishing Company, 2003.

Solomon, Brian, and Mike Schafer. *New York Central Railroad.* Osceola, Wis.: MBI Publishing Company, 1999.

Starr, John W., Jr. *One Hundred Years of American Railroading.* Millersburg, Pa.: Dodd, Mead & Company, 1927.

Staufer, Alvin F. *Pennsy Power III.* Medina, Ohio: A. F. Staufer, 1993.

Staufer, Alvin F., with Philip Shuster and Eugene L. Huddleston. *C&O Power.* Carrollton, Ohio: Alvin F. Staufer, 1965.

Stevens, Frank W. *The Beginnings of the New York Central Railroad.* New York: Putnam, 1926.

Stover, John F. *The Life and Decline of the American Railroad.* New York: Oxford University Press, 1970.

———. *History of the Illinois Central Railroad.* New York: MacMillan, 1975.

———. *History of the Baltimore & Ohio Railroad.* West Lafayette, Ind.: Purdue University Press, 1987.

———. *The Routledge Historical Atlas of the American Railroads.* New York: Routledge, 1999.

Taber, Thomas Townsend. *The Delaware, Lackawanna & Western Railroad: The Route of the* Phoebe Snow *in the Twentieth Century, 1899–1960.* Williamsport, Pa.: T. T. Taber III, 1980.

Taber, Thomas Townsend, and Thomas Townsend Taber III. *The Delaware, Lackawanna & Western Railroad in the Twentieth Century, Vol II.* Williamsport, Pa.: T. T. Taber III, 1981.

Teichmoeller, John. *Pennsylvania Railroad Steel Open Hopper Cars.* Aurora, Colo.: Highland Stations, 2000.

Thompson, Slason. *Short History of American Railways.* Chicago: Bureau of Railway News and Statistics, 1925.

Trewman, H. F. *Electrification of Railways.* London, 1920.

Vance, James E., Jr. *The North American Railroad: Its Origin, Evolution and Geography.* Baltimore: The Johns Hopkins University Press, 1995.

Walker, Mike. *Steam Powered Video's Comprehensive Railroad Atlas of North America: North East U.S.A.* Feaversham, Kent, U.K.: Steam Powered Publishing, 1993.

Westing, Frederic, and Alvin F. Staufer. *Erie Power.* Medina, Ohio: A. F. Staufer, 1970.

White, John H., Jr. *A History of the American Locomotive: Its Development, 1830–1880.* Baltimore: The John Hopkins University Press, 1968.

White, John H., Jr. *American Railroad Freight Car.*

———. *Early American Locomotives.* Toronto: Dover Publications, 1979.

White, Roy V., and A. C. Loudon. *Car Builders Dictionary.* New York: Simmons-Boardman, 1916.

Williams, Harold A. *The Western Maryland Railway Story.* Baltimore: Western Maryland Railway Company, 1952.

Winchester, Clarence. *Railway Wonders of the World, Vols. 1 & 2.* London: Amalgamated Press, 1935.

Yates, John A. *Standard Specifications for Railroad & Canal Construction.* Chicago: The Railway Age Publishing Company, 1886.

Zimmermann, Karl R. *Erie Lackawanna East.* New York: Quadrant Press, 1975.

Zollitsch, Mike. *Buffalo, Rochester & Pittsburgh Railway Volume 2: Pennsylvania-Middle Division.* Scotch Plains, N.J.: Morning Sun Books, 2007.

Periodicals

Baldwin Locomotives. Philadelphia, Pa. (no longer published).

Coal Age. Denver, Colo.

CTC Board: Railroads Illustrated. Ferndale, Wash.

Diesel Era. Halifax, Pa.

Electric Light & Power. Tulsa, Okla.

Jane's World Railways. London.

Keystone Coal Buyers Manual, New York.

Locomotive & Railway Preservation. Waukesha, Wis. (no longer published).

Official Guide to the Railways. New York.

RailNews. Waukesha, Wis. (no longer published).

Railpace Newsmagazine. Piscataway, N.J.

Railroad History (formerly *Railway and Locomotive Historical Society Bulletin*). Boston.

Railway Age. Chicago and New York.

Railway Gazette. New York (1870–1908).

Railway Signaling and Communications (formerly *The Railway Signal Engineer,* nee *Railway Signaling*). Chicago and New York (no longer published).

The Railway Gazette. London.

Trains. Waukesha, Wis.

Vintage Rails. Waukesha, Wis. (no longer published).

Washington Post. Washington, D.C.

Brochures, Catalogs, Manuals, Pamphlets, Rule Books, and Timetables

The Bullsheet.

Burlington Northern Santa Fe Corporation. *Annual Reports 1996–2004.*

Burlington Northern Santa Fe Railway. Grade profiles, (nd).

Burlington Northern Santa Fe Railway. System map, 2003.

CSX Transportation. Baltimore Division Timetable No. 2, 1987.

CSX Transportation. System map, 1999.

Conrail. Pittsburgh Division Timetable No. 5, 1997.

Delaware, Lackawanna & Western. *A Manual of the Delaware, Lackawanna & Western*, 1928.

Erie Railroad. *Erie Railroad: Its Beginnings and Today*, 1951.

Proceedings of the Institution of Mechanical Engineers. *Diesel Locomotives for the Future*, 1987.

Somerset Railroad Corporation. Timetable No. 2, 1990.

Steamtown National Historic Site. *The Nation's Living Railroad Museum*, (nd).

Switchback Gravity Railroad Foundation. *The Route of the Switch Back: A Walker's Tour*, 1997.

The Monongahela Railway. *Timetable No. 5*, 1985.

Reports and Unpublished Works

Clemensen, A. Berle. *Historic Research Study: Steamtown National Historic Site Pennsylvania*. Denver: U.S. Department of the Interior, 1988.

National Park Service. *Historic American Engineering Record: Steamtown National Historic Site, Pennsylvania*. Washington, D.C.: U.S. Department of the Interior, 1989.

Internet

American Meteorological Society

Arch Coal

Association of American Railroads

BNSF Railway

Brotherhood of Locomotive Engineers and Trainmen

CONSOL Energy

U.S. Environmental Protection Agency

Union Pacific Railroad

Index